PROBLEMS OF THE MODERN ECONOMY

Private Wants and Public Needs

PROBLEMS OF THE MODERN ECONOMY

General Editor: EDMUND S. PHELPS, *Columbia University*

Each volume in this series presents
prominent positions in the debate of
an important issue of economic policy

THE BATTLE AGAINST UNEMPLOYMENT

CHANGING PATTERNS IN FOREIGN TRADE
AND PAYMENTS

THE GOAL OF ECONOMIC GROWTH

MONOPOLY POWER AND ECONOMIC PERFORMANCE

PRIVATE WANTS AND PUBLIC NEEDS

THE UNITED STATES AND THE DEVELOPING ECONOMIES

LABOR AND THE NATIONAL ECONOMY

INEQUALITY AND POVERTY

DEFENSE, SCIENCE, AND PUBLIC POLICY

AGRICULTURAL POLICY IN AN AFFLUENT SOCIETY

THE CRISIS OF THE REGULATORY COMMISSIONS

Private Wants
and Public Needs

ISSUES SURROUNDING THE SIZE AND
SCOPE OF GOVERNMENT EXPENDITURE

Edited with an introduction by
EDMUND S. PHELPS
University of Pennsylvania

REVISED EDITION

NEW YORK
W · W · NORTON & COMPANY · INC ·

"Standards and Values in a Rich Society": from *The American Economy* by Alvin H. Hansen. Copyright 1957 by McGraw-Hill Book Company. Reprinted by permission of McGraw-Hill Book Company.

"The Dependence Effect and Social Balance": from *The Affluent Society* by John Kenneth Galbraith (Boston: Houghton Mifflin Company, 1958). Reprinted by permission of the publishers.

"The Non Sequitur of the 'Dependence Effect' " by F. A. Hayek: from the *Southern Economic Journal* (April 1961). Reprinted by permission of the author and the *Journal*.

"Public versus Private: Could Galbraith Be Wrong?" by Henry C. Wallich: from *Harper's Magazine* (October 1961) and from *The Cost of Freedom* by Henry C. Wallich, copyright © 1960 by the author. Reprinted by permission of the author and Harper and Row, Publishers.

"On State Expenditures": from *The Ethics of Redistribution* by Bertrand de Jouvenel. Published by the Cambridge University Press. Reprinted by permission of the publishers.

"Why the Government Budget Is Too Small" by Anthony Downs: from *World Politics* (July 1960). Reprinted by permission.

"The Economic Functions of the State in English Classical Political Economy": from *The Theory of Economic Policy* by Lionel Robbins. Published by Macmillan and Company Ltd. Reprinted by permission of the author, the publishers, St Martin's Press, Inc., and the Macmillan Company of Canada Ltd.

"The Role of Government in a Free Society": Chapter II from *Capitalism and Freedom* by Milton Friedman (Chicago, 1962). Reprinted by permission of The University of Chicago Press.

"Government and the Sovereign Consumer": from *The Question of Government Spending* by Francis M. Bator. Copyright © 1960 by the author. Reprinted by permission of Harper and Row, Publishers.

"Prices vs. Taxes: A Classification of U. S. Public Expenditures": from *Public Finances: Needs, Sources and Utilization* by O. H. Brownlee. Copyright © 1961 by the Princeton University Press. Reprinted by permission of the publishers.

"The Economics of Urban Renewal": a synopsis of the article by Otto A. Davis and Andrew B. Whinston from *Law and Contemporary Problems* (winter 1961). Reprinted by permission.

Acknowledgments

In the preparation of this volume I have benefited from the criticism and suggestions of many colleagues and students to whom I am grateful. I would like also to thank Robert Harlow for helping to prepare the list of further readings, and Mrs. Merle E. Hochman and Mrs. Sally S. Harrison for their assistance in preparing the book for publication.

E. S. P.

ISBN 0 393 09496 0

PRINTED IN THE UNITED STATES OF AMERICA

Contents

Introduction

EVERYONE RECOGNIZES the need for ground rules governing the operation of the private economy. Governments—federal, state, and local—are generally counted on to enforce contracts, sanction private property, outlaw theft, regulate business, and intervene to some degree in the distribution of the yield of private economic activity. It would be wrong to suggest that there are no longer live issues surrounding the performance of these functions. The extent to which governments exert control on the individual is a source of recurrent debate; people do express their continuing interest in the distribution of income, particularly their share in the total tax burden and in the benefits (transfers) disbursed to individuals by the public sector. But if governments confined themselves to carrying out regulatory or housekeeping operations, controversy over the proper role of the public sector in the economy would be far milder than it is today. All production would have to pass the test of market demand. Goods which consumers would not buy would be unprofitable and not be produced. The nation's output would be produced and distributed by private enterprise, for private profit. Every man's employer (neglecting the handful of public employees busy regulating) would be just another private citizen, like himself. In any basic sense, ours would be a "free enterprise" system.

This is not the system we have. Alongside the private-enterprise sector there has grown up a *public sector* that supplies the community with a great many services. To provide these services the public sector now purchases over one-fifth of the Gross National Product—the market value of all goods and services produced by the economy. Whether these public purchases are from private firms who do the producing or whether the public sector employs resources to do its own producing, the consequence is clear: Much of the nation's production is directly determined not by consumer decisions but by government.

These facts will hardly surprise the contemporary observer. Yet the present-day importance of the public sector could hardly have been dreamed of fifty or even twenty-five years ago. The table below describes how rapidly government expenditures and employment have grown.

Expansion of the U.S. Public Sector

	1900	1925	1937	1950	1962
Government expenditures on goods and services (1962 prices)					
In billions of dollars	7.3	20.8	33.4	57.9	117.0
In percent of Gross National Product	9.4	11.3	15.5	15.5	21.2
Government employment					
In millions of persons	1.4	3.2	4.3	8.0	12.0
In percent of total labor force:					
Federal	1.4	1.8	2.2	5.7	7.0
Civilian	1.1	1.4	1.7	3.1	3.1
Military	.3	.4	.5	2.6	3.9
State and Local	3.5	5.3	5.7	6.6	9.1
Total	4.9	7.1	7.9	12.4	16.1

Note.—All 1962 data are preliminary, seasonally adjusted estimates for the first half of the year. Expenditure data are at annual rates.

SOURCES: Solomon Fabricant, *The Trend of Government Activity in the United States since 1900* (National Bureau of Economic Research, 1952); John W. Kendrick, *Productivity Trends in the United States* (National Bureau of Economic Research, 1961); U.S. Department of Commerce, *Survey of Current Business;* U.S. Department of Labor, *Monthly Labor Review.*

And there are contentions heard that the public sector has only begun to fill the need for public services. This remarkable expansion of the public sector and the popular pressures surrounding it have made government expenditures the center of controversy concerning the role of government and public policy. Are public expenditures too large? Too small? By what principles should we decide the magnitude of government expenditures? Is the scope of the existing expenditure programs too broad and an encroachment on private enterprise? Or is the public sector neglecting needs which it alone can effectively satisfy? On what criteria should governments decide whether to supply a service? The essays collected here debate these central questions.

SIZE AND SCOPE OF PUBLIC EXPENDITURE

The volume is divided into two parts. The essays of Part One express a variety of positions on the present size and scope of public expenditures in this country. From the economic view-point, there is on one side the contention that many government expenditures are unnecessary or too large and therefore wasteful of the nation's still-scarce resources; this is countered, on the opposite side, by the argument that while the country is lavishly supplied with private consumer goods, it has skimped irrationally on the kinds of services which can only (or can best) be supplied by government. From the political viewpoint, opposing sides in the debate are taken by those who maintain that the public sector has usurped functions and responsibilities which were better left to the individual business firm, the family, and other valued private institutions, and those who argue that the present range of choices before us is too narrow to pose any grand ideological issues.

One of the most eloquent champions of an expanded role for the public sector is Alvin H. Hansen. His essay calls for a change of values away from materialism and commercialism toward a more intellectually and spiritually satisfying life. Government is viewed as an essential instrument to promote the cultural development of the country. Hansen makes a special plea for greater effort in the field of education. This is essential to raise the "submerged tenth" of the population to a decent standard of living.

Hansen takes it for granted that the public is getting less from the public sector than it really wants. Yet it might have been supposed that in our democratic society decisions regarding the public sector serve the best interests of the citizenry.

John Kenneth Galbraith makes explicit his view that the public is being systematically misled into alloting too little to the public sector. He builds most of this argument around what he calls the "dependence effect." As a society becomes affluent, Galbraith argues, wants begin to take on a relative nature: they increase with the increasing capacity to satisfy them. Through the processes of emulation and advertising, wants come to depend on output. Therefore, despite the enormous growth in our capacity to produce, consumers never feel they can release any of this productive capacity, by paying more taxes, for badly needed services. They are caught like mice on a treadmill of ever-growing wants. This irrational response to public needs is reinforced, according to Galbraith, by traditional beliefs that governments are unable to produce anything of economic value. Thus irrationality and tradition conspire to promote what Galbraith regards as a patent

imbalance between the public and private sectors. On this socio-
logical evidence Galbraith asserts that economic welfare would
be increased more by an expansion of government expenditures
than by an expansion of consumer expenditures.

F. A. Hayek takes issue with the dependence-effect argument.
All but the most basic wants are conditioned by the cultural
environment. But this is no reason to conclude that additional
consumer expenditures would be worthless or inferior to public
spending. There was no visible demand for the novels of C. P.
Snow before they were produced; but this does not make them
ipso facto of low urgency.

Hency C. Wallich offers another criticism of Galbraith's argument. If consumers spend badly, he argues, then better private
spending seems on the face to be indicated, not more government
spending—of which there is already quite a little. He asks whether
there are not powerful biases—logrolling is an example—working in the opposite direction, toward swollen government budgets.
In addition, Wallich objects to the treatment of the public expenditure question as a purely economic problem. Where the
product of the public sector is well differentiated from the output
of the private sector—such as defense—the question is indeed
one of how best to allocate resources among competing ends.
But many of the "new needs" are now being satisfied to a degree
—and give prospects of being satisfied with increasing effectiveness—by private enterprise. In these cases the question of government spending becomes a political one, a question of competing means, not competing ends. Here the value of freedom
must be considered.

Wallich also worries that an expansion of public services in
order to meet these new needs would weaken individual incentives to work. In the next essay, George F. Break summarizes his
study of the influence of taxation upon the supply of effort. He
finds no convincing evidence that high taxes have reduced effort
thus far in this country. A possible explanation of this apparent
constancy of effort, Break points out, is that a rise of income and
sales tax rates exerts two opposing effects on effort: the *substitution* effect tempts the taxpayer to work less because each extra
day of work now yields him less additional after-tax buying power.
But this is countered by an *income* effect that tempts the taxpayer
to work harder and longer at the expense of leisure in order to
earn more before-tax income. By earning more he can avoid hav-

ing to cut his budget for private consumption by the full amount of the tax; he can divide the loss between consumption and leisure so as to lessen its burden. If the income effect is strong enough to offset the substitution effect, then effort, on this theory, will rise rather than fall as a result of a tax-financed government expenditure.*

The essay by Bertrand de Jouvenal extends and elaborates an important argument of Wallich's. As the transfer of functions to the public sector continues, he argues, many private institutions find themselves without responsibilities. A family need no longer support the education of its children; as a result the integrity of the family will suffer, if not education. Patrons of the arts and sciences will no longer be needed, and the diversity and imaginativeness of art and science may be lost in the process.

In the final essay of Part One, Anthony Downs argues that public expenditure is always too small in a democracy because the citizen, quite rationally, does not take the time to assess the full benefits of most public expenditure programs, while he is well aware of the costs of government programs. The result is a bias against public programs which is unlikely to be offset, Downs argues, by logrolling.

Essential as the debate in Part One is, it raises some unanswered questions. Many of the public needs that have been foremost in the debate would involve the government in new fields of activity. By what criteria should productive tasks be divided between government and business? What makes some needs best satisfied by private enterprise and others best met by the public sector?

Where a task can be filled with equal efficiency by government and by private enterprise, the choice can be made purely on political grounds. In such cases, this country has generally chosen private enterprise. Thus the presence of large government expenditures in our economy, with its pronounced favoring of

---

* But such an outcome does not imply that society escapes the deadweight welfare loss to which incentive-distorting income and sales taxes generally lead. Ideally all taxes would be unrelated to effort and to consumption so that after-tax wage rates reflected the productivity (in terms of private consumption) of an extra day's work; then public expenditures would have only an income effect tending to increase effort. But governments have to rely mainly on income and sales taxes. Their consequent substitution effect makes effort smaller than it ought to be, whether or not effort rises on balance due to the income effect. Yet the resulting welfare loss may be negligible in relation to the other costs and benefits of public expenditures.

private enterprise, requires an explanation. Part Two of this volume, which is a brief survey of the developments in "public expenditure theory," helps provide such an explanation.

ECONOMIC PURPOSES OF PUBLIC SPENDING

Some simple answers to the question "why government?" come fairly easily. It is traditional to say that we need governments to do those things for the people which they cannot do for themselves. How do we explain these implied inadequacies of the private marketplace (so-called "market failures") when private enterprise is able to do other things so well? And what if private initiative can do the job only at enormous cost? A framework of analysis seems to be needed.

Galbraith, who did not dwell long on the problem, states that the characteristic which divides goods bought by individuals and goods supplied to them by the public sector is a "technical one." "The things which could be taken over and sold for a price were taken over by private producers. Those that could not, but which were in the end no less urgent for that reason, remained with the state." In Part Two we ask: what properties make a good unsaleable yet needed? How do we distinguish between unsaleability because of little demand and unsaleability for intrinsic, technical reasons? Do national defense and weather forecasts have something in common? Television? Education? TVA?

The first selection, by Lionel, Lord Robbins, reveals that the English classical political economists had no articulate theory of the roles of government expenditure. And, far from being doctrinaire concerning the scope of government, the English "classicals" like Smith and Bentham were utilitarian and pragmatic. The only criterion which government activity had to meet was that it promote economic welfare.

Economists are now able to present a systematic treatment of the conditions under which governments must intervene with expenditures and subsidies if a competitive market economy is to achieve a welfare maximum. Milton Friedman states that public expenditures may be justified where there is a "natural" or "technical" monopoly or where there are "neighborhood effects" (or "externalities" to use the technical term).

The next essay, by Francis M. Bator, provides a more detailed (and slightly different) statement of modern doctrine. Bator identifies two cases of "market failures" which call for public expenditure: the case of "decreasing costs" in which private firms, if they set price equal to marginal cost of production (as they should in an ideal economy), cannot break even despite enough consumer demand to justify production; and the case of "public goods"—goods which should be supplied at a zero price because, by their nature, they can be feasibly shared by two or more consumers at no more social cost than the cost of supplying one consumer. (Public goods represent a kind of externality in that one individual is affected by the consumption of public goods by others. Bator neglects nonpublic goods which have "external" effects.) Bator then examines the kinds of services which governments in the United States actually do provide. He finds that these services are overwhelmingly of such a nature—namely, decreasing-cost or public-good—that only the public sector can be expected to supply them at appropriate prices.

In a related study, O. H. Brownlee allocates all government-expenditure programs into three categories: public goods, goods with important neighborhood effects (other than public goods), and goods for which at least some price should be charged (a category that includes most decreasing-cost goods). Much the same conclusions as Bator's can be drawn. Yet Brownlee empha-sizes that while government must subsidize many services, it need not supply all of them free of charge. Nor does the need to finance certain services imply the need for governments to administer them. He summarizes the controversial proposal by Friedman that education be produced and sold privately, with governments merely footing the bill, rather than engaging in the "production" of education.

The next essay provides a nice example of how externalities or neighborhood effects may necessitate public expenditure or at least public regulation if a welfare maximum is to be achieved. Otto A. Davis and Andrew B. Whinston show, using the payoff matrix of game theory, how "urban blight" can arise and they discuss appropriate measures and criteria for urban renewal.

Walter W. Heller appraises the "theory" of public expenditure presented by Friedman and Bator and finds it wanting in certain respects. He does not accept the doctrine that governments do or should confine themselves to the provision of decreasing-cost or externality-producing goods. In many cases, the public provision of certain goods is the most practical means to redistribute income.

Last, George J. Stigler considers the extent to which economic functions assigned to the public sector can be performed adequately by states and localities where grass-roots control is greatest. To what extent are small government units inefficient? How often do the benefits of state and local action spill over boundaries with the result that many local functions are undersupplied from a national viewpoint? Stigler would give each governmental task to the smallest unit which can efficiently perform it.

A few concluding remarks concerning the scope of this volume: We are considering here only government expenditures in the strict sense of the word, that is, only purchases of commodities and services by governmental units and their agencies. This excludes "transfer payments" by governments—payments for which no service has been rendered, to which no strings are attached. To be sure, these transfers raise many of the same issues raised by public expenditures: high taxes, redistribution of income, and so forth. But, unlike expenditures, they do not directly reallocate resources in the economy. Thus they do not interfere with consumer sovereignty, nor with free enterprise in any fundamental sense.

Second, we have not considered the use of government expenditures for anti-cyclical purposes. With respect to combating short-term fluctuations, one can say that this volume is concerned with the average level of government expenditures over the cycle; their variation or timing over the course of the business cycle is another matter. With respect to combating a deeper-seated tendency toward depression, we suppose that measures designed to raise private expenditures, such as tax reductions and easy money, are roughly as effective as increased public expenditures. Similarly, with respect to inflationary tendencies, one has the option to cut private expenditures or public expenditures. Unemployment and inflation depend upon the intensity with which we use (or try to use) our resources, not primarily upon the sector (public or private) where the resources are employed or to which their output is sold. Once the total level of expenditures has been decided, the choice between public and private expenditure must be faced. That is what makes it essentially an economic problem.

PART ONE Private *vs.* Public Spending

Standards and Values in a Rich Society

ALVIN H. HANSEN

Alvin H. Hansen is Lucius N. Littauer Professor of Political Economy Emeritus at Harvard University. His book The American Economy, *in which this essay first appeared, appraises government economic policy in the United States since the war.*

THE ERADICATION OF POVERTY

IT IS not enough to rescue economics, as Keynes sought to do, from the narrow role assigned to it by Marshall—essentially a branch of business cost accounting—and restore it to the loftier plane of Political Economy or, as Adam Smith so aptly put it—The Wealth of Nations. Economics must concern itself with something more than merely maximum output and full employment. It must also concern itself with social priorities. In other words, it must, in a sense, become a branch of moral philosophy, as Adam Smith indeed had it.

In the last half-century the American Economy has lifted the standard of living of the mass population to undreamed-of levels of comfort and luxury. Mass poverty has largely been wiped out.

Income per family in real terms is now about two and a half times as high as at the beginning of this century. This represents a gain in real purchasing power of 1¾ per cent per annum. At the same time working hours have been reduced from around 60 per week to 40 per week; from a ten-hour day and a six-day week to an eight-hour day and a five-day week. The gain in leisure time is clearly one of the best indices of a higher standard of living.

Still the impressive rise in purchasing-power income requires at least some qualification. A calculation based on money income and price changes is not altogether convincing. In the nineteenth-century rural society many things were free which we now have to pay for. Consider the amount of labor which must be devoted in modern communities, not to positive productive effort, but to neutralizing the disagreeable consequences of dense concentrations of population in large urban communities. Much effort is devoted, not to providing utilities, but to the removal of dis-utilities, by-products of industrialization and urbanization. Yet the labor expended on the removal of disutilities is counted in our money economy as a part of our Gross National Product.

Industrialized cities with overcrowded tenement districts have made an effort via public parks to recover *some* of the lost sunshine, open fields, and fresh air formerly enjoyed by rural populations. Yet in many communities the parks are not located where people live, where children can have direct access to them. Instead of big and grand parks we need many small neighborhood parks, not for an outing but for daily use, not for an occasional automobile drive but for continuous recreation.

Thus it is that our ugly industrial cities scarcely help to build up a convincing case that our standard of living is as far above that of fifty or a hundred years ago as the figures of money incomes corrected for price changes would indicate. In 1900, 60 per cent of our population lived in rural areas and only 22 per cent in cities of over 25,000. Now only 40 per cent live in rural areas, and 60 million people live in cities of over 25,000. The terrific problems of providing urban transportation involve a vast investment of capital and labor. And while the work week is far shorter, should we not add back some part of the hours spent in the nerve-racking rush to get to and from work? In these terms there are still many people who have what in fact amounts to a ten-hour day.

HOUSING AND EDUCATION

The American people are certainly better housed now than fifty years ago. Plumbing, electric lights, and central heating are indicative of this advance. Yet even today we have over 7 million substandard dwelling units which ought at once to be demolished, either because they are without toilet, bath, running water, or are otherwise dilapidated. Kerosene stoves still heat a high proportion of the homes in many working-class sections—a major cause of fires. To complete the task of raising housing standards to the minimum of decency for all would require, it is estimated by the Twentieth Century Fund,[1] around $85 billion. There is still a good deal of unfinished business before we can say that the American people are well housed. Nonetheless, there is a vast difference between the housing facilities available to the American wage-earning family today compared with the situation around 1890, when Jacob Riis gave his lurid description of *How the Other Half Lives.*

So familiar have we become with the widespread use of electrical household appliances that we are prone to think that all Americans are now equipped with these comforts. Yet 50 per cent do not have vacuum cleaners, 30 per cent do not have electric washing machines, and 20 per cent are without electric refrigerators.[2] Still, apart from food and housing and more leisure time, the most conspicuous gains, no doubt, for the great majority are the mechanical gadgets, comforts, and luxuries—household appliances, plumbing, the automobile, the motion picture, radio, and television.

The substitution of mechanical power for human power and the consequent gains in productivity have not only reduced the work week from 60 to 40 hours; they have also made possible a much longer period of education for the whole population. In this respect we have witnessed a truly revolutionary development since 1900, indeed since 1910. As late as 1910 only 5 per cent of the youth of college age (18 to 21) attended college. By 1950 it was 30 per cent.[3] As late as 1910 only a few went on to high school. Then the flood began. Already by 1920 high-school graduations per capita had doubled, and by 1940 the number graduating from high school each year was, per capita, eight times that of 1900. And by 1950 the number of graduations from colleges

1. *America's Needs and Resources,* Twentieth Century Fund, 1955, p. 512.
2. *Ibid.,* p. 242.
3. James B. Conant, *Education and Liberty,* Harvard University, 1953, p. 35.

and universities, on a per capita basis, had reached eight times that of 1900.

Nothing else like it has occurred in any other part of the world. We have not had time to make the proper adjustments. This flood of students into secondary schools and higher institutions has come upon us in a single generation. It is no wonder that our high-school standards are low. No nation could train an adequate number of competent teachers in so short a time. Worse yet, we have miserably failed to give teachers the salary differential needed to draw the best brains into the teaching profession. On the stage we ridicule schoolma'ams, and in the market place we underprice them.

The task of education is, moreover, enormously complicated by the heterogeneity of our population and the difficult problem of immigrant adjustment to American life. Forty-five million immigrants have stormed our shores during the last hundred years. In 1900, 40 per cent of the whole population was foreign-born, or born of foreign parents, and the figure is still 25 per cent today.

THE SUBMERGED TENTH

This mass immigration explains in no small measure the extraordinary spread between the median income in the United States and the income of the lowest decile. And it accounts in considerable degree for many personal and family maladjustments and social dislocations.

What was it that caused this massive movement of people from the Old World to the New? It was primarily the revolutionary increase in population which occurred in Europe throughout the nineteenth century. From 1800 to 1910 the population of the five largest European countries—England, France, Italy, Germany, and Russia—increased from 125 million to 325 million. The chief cause was the sharp decline in the death rate. The struggle for existence grew desperate. Subdivision of the family plots pushed down the subsistence level. Peasants by the millions were forced off the land. In America they crowded, after the 1880s, into our great urban industrial centers. Uprooted from their Old World peasant communities, where human ties were close and moral values were firmly fixed, they were all at sea in a new and strange world. The uprooted immigrant had to readjust his peasant outlook on life.[4] He had to come to terms with an urbanized industrialism.

To make matters still worse, a psychological conflict, placing severe strains on parental discipline, inevitably developed between the immigrant and his children—a conflict born of differences in language and social environment. The restraints and security of the Old World peasant communities were missing. Sheds, shanties, stables, and cellars were drafted for living space in our great industrial centers. The crowded street was the only playground.[5] Out of such conditions have grown psychopathic disorders and social maladjustments. It is true that those endowed with exceptional energy and capacity, both mental and physical, found in the American environment almost boundless opportunities and rose very rapidly to higher social and economic levels. More gradually the great middle group also improved its status and succeeded reasonably well in the difficult process of amalgamation and assimilation. But there was also the submerged tenth or quintile.

The physical and mental deficiencies which we find today among the lower two deciles of our population stem in part at least from the conflicts experienced by the uprooted peasant immigrant unable to find his way about in congested cities amid the uncertainties and insecurity of a laissez-faire industrialism. Against the background of these conditions one can learn a good deal that explains the submerged decile in a rich society.

In the United States today there are 8,000,000 families and individual household units with a money income of less than $1,000 per year and an additional 6,500,000 with incomes between $1,000 and $2,000. A considerable proportion live in depressed areas, where unemployment is chronic even when the nation as a whole is enjoying full-employment opportunities. It is a vicious circle. Because the area is depressed, public revenues are limited. Community services, and especially the quality of education, are seriously deficient. Such areas become not merely economi-

---

4. Oscar Handlin, *The Uprooted,* Little, Brown & Company, 1952.
5. I note even today, as I walk around the streets of some of our great cities, that school children in recess time have frequently no place to play except on pavement and adjoining sidewalks.

cally depressed areas; they become also derelict areas, composed of a population with inferior education and lacking in physical and mental vigor. The able, aggressive young people migrate. Those who remain behind constitute, disproportionately, aged persons, remaining members of broken families, and generally persons inadequately equipped to compete successfully in modern industry.

In part it is a rural problem, and in part it is a race problem. Two-thirds of the low-income rural families live in the South. Moreover, the incidence of low incomes among rural families is twice as great among Negroes as among whites.

Lack of education is a primary cause of low income. Low-income families are compelled to spend a disproportionate per cent of their income on food and housing. There is little left for education. Substandard families spend 65 per cent of their income on food and housing, while wage-earning families in general spend only 45 per cent on these two consumption categories. Moreover, as I have already indicated, such families are likely to live in communities where educational facilities are very limited. About 30 per cent of all the nation's children live in the eighteen lowest-income states. Several of these states have a per capita income less than half that of the richest states.

These poorer states cannot, without substantial Federal aid, provide the minimum American standards of education, health, and social welfare. These children are Americans. Yet citizens of New York and Massachusetts are prone to talk and act as though they were foreigners. We are indeed almost immeasurably distant from being *world* citizens. In the present stage of human development this is at least understandable. But is it not incredible that we pretend to be citizens of our separate states and not citizens of the United States when we consider the problem of adequate minimum standards of education for Americans everywhere?

The wide spread between the median income and the lowest decile in our society holds not only with respect to income and education but also with respect to physical fitness. Not only is the rate of illiteracy high in the lower deciles, but the extraordinary high proportion of our total youth physically and mentally unfit for military service is clearly in some part to be explained by the unfavorable economic and social conditions under which the lower deciles of our population live. Slum clearance and a nationwide system of health insurance are high in the agenda of unfinished business.

It is not only the personal incomes and the physical and mental status of the submerged tenth which are seriously deficient. It is also their opportunity to share in the amenities of life which only the community can offer. Our great cities lack adequate parks and playgrounds—Cambridge, Mass., is a notorious example—and they lack community facilities for recreation and social life. The joy of living in a city with beautiful parks within the reach of all and with easy and quick access to the surrounding countryside is something that our lower-income groups do not share in equal measure with comparable income groups in Holland, Switzerland, Denmark, and Sweden.

Joyful living is not simply an individual matter. Among the more important amenities of life are those which only the community can provide. This is a job for government. And if we hide behind the doctrine that all this is no affair of the Federal government, we become in practice pure defeatists.

The lower-income classes are at a peculiar disadvantage because of the preoccupation of the American society with mechanical gadgets and because of the relatively slight emphasis placed upon social values and community activities. We are increasingly in danger of making our economic system a mere treadmill. We have reached a point in our development where mere emphasis on larger and larger output of mechanical gadgets becomes rather meaningless, if, indeed, not a detriment to truly satisfactory living. We spend billions and billions of dollars on automobiles, of which perhaps half is frittered away on mere size, gadgets, and chrome—all of which add little to the social utility of comfortable transportation. And expenditures on automobiles, not including operation or the vast sums spent on roads, are twice as great as the aggregate expenditure on schools, including school construction and other capital outlays for education.

The average public-school teacher's salary is $3,450, while the average full-time wage for production workers in manufacturing industry is $3,735, and that for railroad production workers (not including supervising employees) is $4,100. A country as rich as ours can and should make the school teacher's profession highly attractive financially. A good rule, and a thoroughly justifiable one, would be an average salary scale twice that of production workers. This means more than a doubling of school teachers' salaries. In ten years we should see a profound change in the quality of our teachers. To say that we can't afford it is nonsense. We are spending currently a paltry $3½ billion on public-school teachers' salaries. We can well afford to double or treble that amount out of our rapidly increasing national income.

We shall not solve the problem of education for the submerged tenth or the lowest quintile until we have solved it for all the people. The same holds for youth programs, recreational facilities, and a nationwide system of health insurance.

WHAT GOALS DO WE SEEK?

After ten years of almost incredible *output* performance, we need to assess not merely the speed of our growth and progress but also the direction in which we are going. What *qualitative* goals shall we set up? What kind of country do we wish to build? These are matters that we dare not overlook, lest we perish, as a great nation, in the midst of material plenty.

Now someone will surely say: "What right has this armchair professor to talk about how the American public should use its resources? Leave it to the market to take care of all that." Superficially that sounds good, but in fact that answer will not do. The "market" cannot decide how much we shall spend on schools, on social security, or on national security. We have reached a point in our economic and social evolution where *social-value* judgments, not the market, must control the uses to which we put something like one-fourth of our productive resources. Our economy is no longer wholly a market economy. It is a mixed public-private economy.

And how are these social-value judgments to be determined? Do we leave it to chance, to nature, to the elemental, uneducated instincts of people? That indeed is the rule among savages. But civilized countries follow another rule, and it is this: "Train up a child in the way he should go, and when he is a man he will not depart therefrom." Civilized countries mold their people into civilized ways of thinking, guided by values that experience and knowledge have laid down. We don't leave it to the market. We educate. Only in this way can we achieve the great goals of a civilized society.

Here I come to a critical point. Our schools and churches can no longer be said to constitute the main educational media in this country. Modern technology has largely supplanted these older media. Children, young people, and grownups devote more hours per day the year round to the radio and television and the movies than they do to school, churches, or to reading. These mechanical media have become an important, if indeed not the most important, element in our entire educational process. And what worries me is this. These powerful educational media are controlled, not by educators, but by advertisers whose primary purpose is profit, not education. Advertisers do not control the editorials or news columns of our newspapers, though there may be an indirect influence. But they do control our radio and television programs. Is it any wonder that we prefer longer and longer cars with more and more chrome to good schools and well-paid teachers? At the very least, advertisers should not, I suggest, be allowed to sponsor or select the programs other than their own commercials.

We have been brought up with a narrow conception of the functions of public education. Adult education, music, drama, the fine arts, deserve public support. Even our F.M. fine music programs are painfully encroached upon by advertising.

Thus the problem of social priorities is hard upon us. It is not enough to achieve maximum employment and production. It is not enough to have quantitative goals. We cannot allow full employment to become merely a device to make our economy an efficient treadmill.

America's Needs and Resources discloses (p. 512) that the estimated cost of urban redevelopment in general—including a demolition of our 7 million slum houses—would amount to no more than the equivalent of about two years of defense expenditures at current levels.

In terms of GNP we are spending currently only 40 per cent as much on hospitals today as in 1920–1924 (p. 312). We are spending (including operating and capital expenditures) only

2¼ per cent of our GNP on public schools, elementary and secondary. Indeed, in relation to GNP we are spending 20 per cent less on schools today than we spent twenty-five years ago. A rich country can't afford good schools and good teachers!

This is an area in which economists have been, I feel, neglectful of their duty. We need more study of social priorities.

Yet with all our distorted values there is happily a growing realization that we *have* accumulated a large backlog of long-range public-investment needs. This means larger and larger Federal budgets, not only absolutely but also in relation to the GNP. When I say "public investment" I mean not merely public works and resource-development projects. I include investment in human resources as well—schools, scholarship programs, medical research, a nationwide system of health insurance, recreational facilities, etc.

The problem of long-range public-investment planning is all the more important in view of our large and now again increasing defense and foreign-aid budgets. The national-security budgets compete with the growing urgent need for much larger long-range social-welfare budgets. I think we should all agree that national security comes first. Indeed I have never been able to understand why we continually debate the question whether our military strength is more or less equal to that of the Soviet Union when we, in fact, have ample resources to ensure our superiority by a wide margin. Our military program should be adequate to guarantee without question the peace of the world for the visible future. I am not, therefore, suggesting that we should reduce our military program. But I do, nonetheless, say that we should increase *now* by a substantial amount our long-range public-welfare budgets. That may involve a reappraisal of tax cuts. We are in a situation in which the marginal *tax* dollar can clearly yield a much higher social utility than the marginal *pay-envelope* dollar.

Let it be noted that the growing ratio of government purchases of goods and services—a trend which has been going on throughout our history—does indeed point up the unmistakable *fact* that our economy is becoming more and more a mixed public-private economy. But government ownership and operation of the means of production—the classical definition of socialism—is *not* noticeably on the increase. It is the welfare state that is growing, not the government as owner or operator. The welfare state is primarily a redistributor of income and a colossal purchaser of the products of private enterprise. But private enterprise does the job.

The growth of public budgets means that the public *finance* method of paying for goods and services will grow in relation to the *market-price* method. It does not mean that private enterprise is shrinking or that the tax base is shrinking. The goods are purchased from private enterprise. Thus private enterprise continues to grow in much the same proportion as the GNP. The welfare state does not in any appreciable degree operate to supplant the system of private enterprise. Instead it makes it stronger and more workable.

No one can dispute that we have become a rich society. We have made great advances on the purely economic plane. Unfortunately the progress we have made in many of the noneconomic aspects of life is limited, and in some areas we have, I fear, definitely retrogressed. The economic gains are visible on every hand. And economists, as a professional group, have, I think it is fair to say, contributed in no small measure to this development. Government departments have at long last been staffed with well-trained economists. State papers nowadays are mainly concerned with economic matters, often highly technical. Congressional hearings and legislative programs draw increasingly on the work of economists inside and outside the government. The result is evident in the massive and highly technical messages and reports of the President to Congress.

Would that our colleagues, concerned with noneconomic aspects of American life, could claim equal progress. We are learning, in the midst of material plenty, that man "cannot live by bread alone." How do educators feel when they contemplate the deterioration of our public schools; the social psychologists and pathologists who observe the increase in mental disorders, crime, and juvenile delinquency, or, on another plane, the current predominance of neurotic art?

We have learned how to make a living; we have still to learn how to live. Until we have eliminated the ugliness of our great industrial cities we cannot claim to have reached as a nation a truly high standard of living. America is long on wealth but short on appreciation of the beautiful. Some years ago I visited, in company with Professor Jørgen Pedersen, a large farm in Jutland, Denmark. It employed eighteen or twenty well-housed farm workers. Two of these devoted full time to beautifying the place, to the flower gardens, the lawns, the trees, the buildings. That farm was a place on which to live, not merely a place to make a living.

Many readers have no doubt visited the famous Town Hall in Stockholm, a noble work of man. Compare this with the city hall in Boston, Mass., to take only one example. The Town Hall in Stockholm is not simply a place where the mayor has his office. It is a community building where citizens of high or low rank can meet in civic-group gatherings amidst an atmosphere of dignity, beauty, and elegance. Such things make for the good life. A higher standard of mere material wealth is no substitute for beauty—for the things of the mind and the spirit.

Few will deny the cultural deficiencies of our cities and towns, and everyone will agree that an adequate program would cost a lot of money. And the answer to that usually is that we can't afford it. We are too poor! Ah, that is it. We have become so gadget-rich that we can't afford to build culturally rich communities. But what does it profit a man if he gain the whole world but lose his own soul?

The Dependence Effect and Social Balance

JOHN KENNETH GALBRAITH

John Kenneth Galbraith, Professor of Economics at Harvard University, was formerly United States Ambassador to India. In The Affluent Society, *from which the following essay was taken, Galbraith examines the use to which this country puts its wealth.*

WEALTH IS not without its advantages and the case to the contrary, although it has often been made, has never proved widely persuasive. But, beyond doubt, wealth is the relentless enemy of understanding. The poor man has always a precise view of his problem and its remedy: he hasn't enough and he needs more. The rich man can assume or imagine a much greater variety of ills and he will be correspondingly less certain of their remedy. Also, until he learns to live with his wealth, he will have a well-observed tendency to put it to the wrong purposes or otherwise to make himself foolish.

As with individuals so with nations. And the experience of nations with well-being is exceedingly brief. Nearly all throughout all history have been very poor. The exception, almost insignificant in the whole span of human existence, has been the last few generations in the comparatively small corner of the world populated by Europeans. Here, and especially in the United States, there has been great and quite unprecedented affluence.

The ideas by which the people of this favored part of the world interpret their existence, and in measure guide their behavior, were not forged in a world of wealth. These ideas were the product of a world in which poverty had always been man's normal lot, and any other state was in degree unimaginable. This poverty was not the elegant torture of the spirit which comes from contemplating another man's more spacious possessions. It was the unedifying mortification of the flesh—from hunger, sickness, and cold. Those who might be freed temporarily from such burden could not know when it would strike again, for at best hunger yielded only perilously to privation. It is improbable that the

13

poverty of the masses of the people was made greatly more bearable by the fact that a very few—those upon whose movements nearly all recorded history centers—were very rich.

No one would wish to argue that the ideas which interpreted this world of grim scarcity would serve equally well for the contemporary United States. Poverty was the all-pervasive fact of that world. Obviously it is not of ours. One would not expect that the preoccupations of a poverty-ridden world would be relevant in one where the ordinary individual has access to amenities—foods, entertainment, personal transportation, and plumbing—in which not even the rich rejoiced a century ago. So great has been the change that many of the desires of the individual are no longer even evident to him. They become so only as they are synthesized, elaborated, and nurtured by advertising and salesmanship, and these, in turn, have become among our most important and talented professions. Few people at the beginning of the nineteenth century needed an adman to tell them what they wanted.

It would be wrong to suggest that the economic ideas which once interpreted the world of mass poverty have made no adjustment to the world of affluence. There have been many adjustments including some that have gone unrecognized or have been poorly understood. But there has also been a remarkable resistance. And the total alteration in underlying circumstances has not been squarely faced. As a result we are guided, in part, by ideas that are relevant to another world; and as a further result we do many things that are unnecessary, some that are unwise, and a few that are insane. . . .

THE LOW REPUTE OF PUBLIC PRODUCTION

Our concern for production is traditional and irrational. We are curiously unreasonable in the distinctions we make between different kinds of goods and services. We view the production of some of the most frivolous goods with pride. We regard the production of some of the most significant and civilizing services with regret.

In the general view it is privately produced production that is important, and that nearly alone. This adds to national well-being. Its increase measures the increase in national wealth.

Public services, by comparison, are an incubus. They are necessary, and they may be necessary in considerable volume. But they are a burden which must, in effect, be carried by the private production. If that burden is too great, private production will stagger and fall.

At best public services are a necessary evil; at worst they are a malign tendency against which an alert community must exercise eternal vigilance. Even when they serve the most important ends, such services are sterile. "Government is powerless to create anything in the sense in which business produces wealth. . . ." [1]

Such attitudes lead to some interesting contradictions. Automobiles have an importance greater than the roads on which they are driven. We welcome expansion of telephone services as improving the general well-being but accept curtailment of postal services as signifying necessary economy. We set great store by the increase in private wealth but regret the added outlays for the police force by which it is protected. Vacuum cleaners to insure clean houses are praiseworthy and essential in our standard of living. Street cleaners to insure clean streets are an unfortunate expense. Partly as a result, our houses are generally clean and our streets generally filthy. In the more sophisticated of the conventional wisdom, this distinction between public and private services is much less sharp and, as I have observed, it does not figure in the calculation of Gross National Product. However, it never quite disappears. Even among economists and political philosophers, public services rarely lose their connotation of burden. Although they may be defended, their volume and quality are almost never a source of pride.

There are a number of reasons for these attitudes, but again tradition plays a dominant role. In the world into which economics was born the four most urgent requirements of man were food, clothing, and shelter, and an orderly environment in which the first three might be provided. The first three lent themselves to private production for the market; given good order, this process has ordinarily gone forward with tolerable efficiency. But order which was the gift of government was nearly always

1. Francis X. Sutton, Seymour E. Harris, Carl Kaysen, and James Tobin, *The American Business Creed* (Cambridge, Mass.: Harvard University Press, 1956), p. 195.

supplied with notable unreliability. With rare exceptions it was also inordinately expensive. And the pretext of providing order not infrequently afforded the occasion for rapacious appropriation of the means of sustenance of the people.

Not surprisingly, modern economic ideas incorporated a strong suspicion of government. The goal of nineteenth century economic liberalism was a state which did provide order reliably and inexpensively and which did as little as possible else. Even Marx intended that the state should wither away. These attitudes have persisted in the conventional wisdom. And again events have dealt them a series of merciless blows. Once a society has provided itself with food, clothing, and shelter, all of which so fortuitously lend themselves to private production, purchase, and sale, its members begin to desire other things. And a remarkable number of these things do not lend themselves to such production, purchase, and sale. They must be provided for everyone if they are to be provided for anyone, and they must be paid for collectively or they cannot be had at all. Such is the case with streets and police and the general advantages of mass literacy and sanitation, the control of epidemics, and the common defense. There is a bare possibility that the services which must be rendered collectively, although they enter the general scheme of wants after the immediate physical necessities, increase in urgency more than proportionately with increasing wealth. This is more likely if increasing wealth is matched by increasing population and increasing density of population. Nonetheless these services, although they reflect increasingly urgent desires, remain under the obloquy of the unreliability, incompetence, cost, and pretentious interference of princes. Alcohol, comic books, and mouth wash all bask under the superior reputation of the market. Schools, judges, and municipal swimming pools lie under the evil reputation of bad kings.

Moreover, bad kings in a poorer world showed themselves to be quite capable, in their rapacity, of destroying or damaging the production of private goods by destroying the people and the capital that produced them. Economies are no longer so vulnerable. Governments are not so undiscriminating. In western countries in modern times economic growth and expanding public activity have, with rare exceptions, gone together. Each has served the other as indeed they must. Yet the conventional wisdom is far from surrendering on the point. Any growth in public services is a manifestation of an intrinsically evil trend. If the vigor of the race is not in danger, liberty is. And this may be threatened even by the activities of the local school board. The structure of the economy may also be at stake. In one branch of the conventional wisdom the American economy is never far removed from socialism, and the movement toward socialism may be measured by the rise in public spending. Thus even the most neutral of public services, for one part of the population, fall under the considerable handicap of being identified with social revolution.

Finally—also a closely related point—the payment for publicly produced services has long been linked to the problem of inequality. By having the rich pay more, the services were provided and at the same time the goal of greater equality was advanced. This community of objectives has never appealed to those being equalized. Not unnaturally, some part of their opposition has been directed to the public services themselves. By attacking these, they could attack the leveling tendencies of taxation. This has helped to keep alive the notion that the public services for which they pay are inherently inferior to privately produced goods.

While public services have been subject to these negative attitudes, private goods have had no such attention. On the contrary, their virtues have been extolled by the massed drums of modern advertising. They have been pictured as the ultimate wealth of the community. Clearly the competition between public and private services, apart from any question of the satisfactions they render, is an unequal one. The social consequences of this discrimination—this tendency to accord a superior prestige to private goods and an inferior role to public production—are considerable and even grave.

THE IMPERATIVES OF CONSUMER DEMAND

Both the ancient preoccupation with production and the pervasive modern search for security have culminated in our time in a concern for production. Increased real income provides us with an admirable detour around the rancor anciently associated with efforts to redistribute wealth. A high level of production has become the keystone of effective economic security. There remains, however, the task of justifying the resulting flow of goods. Production cannot be an incidental to the mitigation of inequality or the provision of jobs. It must have a *raison d'être* of its own. At this point economists and economic theory have entered the game. The result has been an elaborate and ingenious defense of the importance of production as such. It is a defense which makes the urgency of production largely independent of the volume of production. In this way economic theory has managed to transfer the sense of urgency in meeting consumer need that once was felt in a world where more production meant more food for the hungry, more clothing for the cold, and more houses for the homeless to a world where increased output satisfies the craving for more elegant automobiles, more exotic food, more erotic clothing, more elaborate entertainment—indeed for the entire modern range of sensuous, edifying, and lethal desires.

Although the economic theory which defends these desires and hence the production that supplies them has an impeccable (and to an astonishing degree even unchallenged) position in the conventional wisdom, it is illogical and meretricious and in degree even dangerous. . . .

In part [the defense by economists] will take the form of a purely assertive posture. "There is still an economic problem"; "We still have poverty"; "It is human nature to want more"; "Without increasing production there will be stagnation"; "We must show the Russians." But the ultimate refuge will remain in the theory of consumer demand. This is a formidable structure; it has already demonstrated its effectiveness in defending the urgency of production. In a world where affluence is rendering the old ideas obsolete, it will continue to be the bastion against the misery of new ones.

The theory of consumer demand, as it is now widely accepted, is based on two broad propositions, neither of them quite explicit but both extremely important for the present value system of economists. The first is that the urgency of wants does not diminish appreciably as more of them are satisfied or, to put the matter more precisely, to the extent that this happens it is not demonstrable and not a matter of any interest to economists or for economic policy. When man has satisfied his physical needs, then psychologically grounded desires take over. These can never be satisfied or, in any case, no progress can be proved. The concept of satiation has very little standing in economics. It is neither useful nor scientific to speculate on the comparative cravings of the stomach and the mind.

The second proposition is that wants originate in the personality of the consumer or, in any case, that they are given data for the economist. The latter's task is merely to seek their satisfaction. He has no need to inquire how these wants are formed. His function is sufficiently fulfilled by maximizing the goods that supply the wants.

The examination of these two conclusions must now be pressed. The explanation of consumer behavior has its ancestry in a much older problem, indeed the oldest problem of economics, that of price determination.[2] Nothing originally proved more troublesome in the explanation of prices, i.e., exchange values, than the indigestible fact that some of the most useful things had the least value in exchange and some of the least useful had the most. As Adam Smith observed: "Nothing is more useful than water; but it will purchase scarce anything; scarce anything can be had in exchange for it. A diamond, on the contrary, has scarce any value in use: but a very great quantity of other goods may frequently be had in exchange for it."[3]

In explaining value, Smith thought it well to distinguish between "value in exchange" and "value in use" and sought thus to reconcile the paradox of high utility and low exchangeability. This distinction begged questions rather than solved them and for another hundred years economists sought for a satisfactory formulation. Finally, toward the end of the last century—though it is now recognized that their work had been extensively anticipated—the three economists of marginal utility (Karl Menger, an Austrian; William Stanley Jevons, an Englishman; and John Bates Clark, an American) produced more or less simultaneously the explanation which in broad substance still serves. The urgency of desire is a function of the quantity of goods which the individual has available to satisfy that desire. The larger the stock the less the satisfactions from an increment. And the less, also, the willingness to pay. Since diamonds for most people are

2. The provenance of the theory of consumer behavior is sketched in Mr. I. D. M. Little's interesting article "A Reformulation of Consumer Behavior," *Oxford Economic Papers*, New Series, vol. 1, no. 1 (January 1949), p. 99.

3. *Wealth of Nations*. Smith did not foresee the industrial diamond.

in comparatively meager supply, the satisfaction from an additional one is great, and the potential willingness to pay is likewise high. The case of water is just the reverse. It also follows that where the supply of a good can be readily increased at low cost, its value in exchange will reflect that ease of reproduction and the low urgency of the marginal desires it thus comes to satisfy. This will be so no matter how difficult it may be (as with water) to dispense entirely with the item in question.

The doctrine of diminishing marginal utility, as it was enshrined in the economics textbooks, seemed to put economic ideas squarely on the side of the diminishing importance of production under conditions of increasing affluence. With increasing per capita real income, men are able to satisfy additional wants. These are of a lower order of urgency. This being so, the production that provides the goods that satisfy these less urgent wants must also be of smaller (and declining) importance. In Ricardo's England the supply of bread for many was meager. The satisfaction resulting from an increment in the bread supply —from a higher money income, bread prices being the same, or the same money income, bread prices being lower—was great. Hunger was lessened; life itself might be extended. Certainly any measure to increase the bread supply merited the deep and serious interest of the public-spirited citizen.

In the contemporary United States the supply of bread is plentiful and the supply of bread grains even redundant. The yield of satisfactions from a marginal increment in the wheat supply is small. To a Secretary of Agriculture it is indubitably negative. Measures to increase the wheat supply are not, therefore, a socially urgent preoccupation of publicly concerned citizens. These are more likely to be found spending their time devising schemes for the effective control of wheat production. And having extended their bread consumption to the point where its marginal utility is very low, people have gone on to spend their income on other things. Since these other goods entered their consumption pattern after bread, there is a presumption that they are not very urgent either—that *their* consumption has been carried, as with wheat, to the point where marginal utility is small or even negligible. So it must be assumed that the importance of marginal increments of all production is low and declining. The effect of increasing affluence is to minimize the importance of economic goals. Production and productivity become less and less important.

The concept of diminishing marginal utility was, and remains, one of the indispensable ideas of economics. Since it conceded so much to the notion of diminishing urgency of wants, and hence of production, it was remarkable indeed that the situation was retrieved. This was done—and brilliantly. The diminishing urgency of wants was not admitted. In part this was accomplished in the name of refined scientific method which, as so often at the higher levels of sophistication, proved a formidable bulwark of the conventional wisdom. Obvious but inconvenient evidence was rejected on the grounds that it could not be scientifically assimilated. But even beyond this, it has been necessary at times simply to close one's eyes to phenomena which could not be reconciled with convenience.

Economics took general cognizance of the fact that an almost infinite variety of goods await the consumer's attention. At the more elementary (and also the more subjective) levels of economic analysis it is assumed that, while the marginal utility of the individual good declines in accordance with the indubitable law, the utility or satisfaction from new and different kinds of goods does not diminish appreciably. So long as the consumer adds new products—seeks variety rather than quantity—he may, like a museum, accumulate without diminishing the urgency of his wants. Since even in Los Angeles the average consumer owns only a fraction of the different kinds of goods he might conceivably possess, there is all but unlimited opportunity for adding such products. The rewards to the possessors are more or less proportional to the supply. The production that supplies these goods and services, since it renders undiminished utility, remains of undiminished importance.

This position ignores the obvious fact that some things are acquired before others and that, presumably, the more important things come first. This, as observed previously, implies a declining urgency of need. However, in the slightly more sophisticated theory this conclusion is rejected. The rejection centers on the denial that anything very useful can be said of the comparative states of mind and satisfaction of the consumer at different periods of time. Few students of economics, even in the elementary course, now escape without a warning against the error of intertemporal comparisons of the utility from given acts of consumption. Yesterday the man with a minimal but increasing real income was reaping the satisfactions which came from a decent diet and a roof that no longer leaked water on his face. Today, after a large increase in his income, he has extended his consumption to include suede shoes and a weekly visit to the races. But to say that his satisfactions from these latter amenities and recreations are less than from the additional calories and the freedom from rain is wholly improper. Things have changed; he is a different man; there is no real standard for comparison. That, as of a given time, an individual will derive lesser satisfactions from the marginal increments to a given stock of goods, and accordingly cannot be induced to pay as much for them, is conceded. But this tells us nothing of the satisfactions from such additional goods, and more particularly from different goods, when they are acquired at a later time. The conclusion follows. One cannot be sure that the satisfaction from these temporally later increases in the individual's stock of goods diminishes. Hence one cannot suggest that the production which supplies it is of diminishing urgency.

A moment's reflection on what has been accomplished will be worth while. The notion of diminishing utility still serves its indispensable purpose of relating urgency of desire and consequent willingness to pay to quantity. At any given time the more the individual might have, the less would be the satisfaction he would derive from additions to his stock and the less he would be willing to pay. The reactions of the community will be the aggregate of the reactions of the individuals it comprises. Hence the greater the supply the less the willingness to pay for marginal increments and hence the demand curve familiar to all who have made even the most modest venture into economic theory. But, at the same time, the question of the diminishing urgency of consumption is elided. For, while the question of willingness to pay for additional quantities is based on a hypothesis as to behavior in face of these quantities at a given point of time, an increase in stock of consumers' goods, as the result of an increase in real income, can occur only over time. On the yield of satisfactions from this the economist has nothing to say. In the name of good scientific method he is prevented from saying anything. There is room, however, for the broad assumption—given the large and ever-growing variety of goods awaiting the consumer's attention—that wants have a sustained urgency. In any case, it can safely be concluded that more goods will satisfy more wants than fewer goods. And the assumption that goods are an important and even an urgent thing to provide stalks unchallenged behind, for have not goods always been important for relieving the privation of mankind? It will be evident that economics has brilliantly retrieved the dangers to itself and to its goals that were inherent in diminishing marginal utility.

There has been dissent. Keynes observed that the needs of human beings "fall into two classes—those needs which are absolute in the sense that we feel them whatever the situation of our fellow human beings may be, and those which are relative only in that their satisfaction lifts us above, makes us feel superior to, our fellows." While conceding that the second class of wants might be insatiable, he argued that the first were capable of being satisfied and went on to conclude that "assuming no important wars and no important increase in population the *economic problem* may be solved, or at least within sight of solution, within a hundred years. This means the economic problem is not—if we look into the future—*the permanent problem of the human race.*" [4] However, on this conclusion Keynes made no headway. In contending with the conventional wisdom he, no less than others, needed the support of circumstance. And in contrast with his remedy for depressions this he did not yet have.

THE DEPENDENCE EFFECT

The notion that wants do not become less urgent the more amply the individual is supplied is broadly repugnant to common sense. It is something to be believed only by those who wish to believe. Yet the conventional wisdom must be tackled on its own terrain. Intertemporal comparisons of an individual's state of mind do rest on doubtful grounds. Who can say for sure that the deprivation which afflicts him with hunger is more painful than the deprivation which afflicts him with envy of his neighbor's new car? In the time that has passed since he was poor his soul may have become subject to a new and deeper searing.

4. J. M. Keynes, *Essays in Persuasion*, "Economic Possibilities for Our Grandchildren," pp. 365–66. The italics are in the original. Notice that Keynes, as always little bound by the conventional rules, did not hesitate to commit the unpardonable sin of distinguishing between categories of desire.

And where a society is concerned, comparisons between marginal satisfactions when it is poor and those when it is affluent will involve not only the same individual at different times but different individuals at different times. The scholar who wishes to believe that with increasing affluence there is no reduction in the urgency of desires and goods is not without points for debate. However plausible the case against him, it cannot be proven. In the defense of the conventional wisdom this amounts almost to invulnerability.

However, there is a flaw in the case. If the individual's wants are to be urgent they must be original with himself. They cannot be urgent if they must be contrived for him. And above all they must not be contrived by the process of production by which they are satisfied. For this means that the whole case for the urgency of production, based on the urgency of wants, falls to the ground. One cannot defend production as satisfying wants if that production creates the wants.

Were it so that a man on arising each morning was assailed by demons which instilled in him a passion sometimes for silk shirts, sometimes for kitchenware, sometimes for chamber pots, and sometimes for orange squash, there would be every reason to applaud the effort to find the goods, however odd, that quenched this flame. But should it be that his passion was the result of his first having cultivated the demons, and should it also be that his effort to allay it stirred the demons to ever greater and greater effort, there would be question as to how rational was his solution. Unless restrained by conventional attitudes, he might wonder if the solution lay with more goods or fewer demons.

So it is that if production creates the wants it seeks to satisfy, or if the wants emerge *pari passu* with the production, then the urgency of the wants can no longer be used to defend the urgency of the production. Production only fills a void that it has itself created.

The point is so central that it must be pressed. Consumer wants can have bizarre, frivolous, or even immoral origins, and an admirable case can still be made for a society that seeks to satisfy them. But the case cannot stand if it is the process of satisfying wants that creates the wants. For then the individual who urges the importance of production to satisfy these wants is precisely in the position of the onlooker who applauds the efforts of the squirrel to keep abreast of the wheel that is propelled by his own efforts.

That wants are, in fact, the fruit of production will now be denied by few serious scholars. And a considerable number of economists, though not always in full knowledge of the implications, have conceded the point. In the observation cited earlier Keynes noted that needs of "the second class," i.e., those that are the result of efforts to keep abreast or ahead of one's fellow being "may indeed be insatiable; for the higher the general level the higher still are they." [5] And emulation has always played a considerable role in the views of other economists of want creation. One man's consumption becomes his neighbor's wish. This already means that the process by which wants are satisfied is also the process by which wants are created. The more wants that are satisfied the more new ones are born.

However, the argument has been carried farther. A leading modern theorist of consumer behavior, Professor Duesenberry, has stated explicitly that "ours is a society in which one of the principal social goals is a higher standard of living. . . . [This] has great significance for the theory of consumption . . . the desire to get superior goods takes on a life of its own. It provides a drive to higher expenditure which may even be stronger than that arising out of the needs which are supposed to be satisfied by that expenditure." [6] The implications of this view are impressive. The notion of independently established need now sinks into the background. Because the society sets great store by ability to produce a high living standard, it evaluates people by the products they possess. The urge to consume is fathered by the value system which emphasizes the ability of the society to produce. The more that is produced the more that must be owned in order to maintain the appropriate prestige. The latter is an important point, for, without going as far as Duesenberry in reducing goods to the role of symbols of prestige in the affluent society, it is plain that his argument fully implies that the production of goods creates the wants that the goods are presumed to satisfy.

The even more direct link between production and wants is provided by the institutions of modern advertising and salesman-

5. *Op. cit.*
6. James S. Duesenberry, *Income, Saving and the Theory of Consumer Behavior* (Cambridge, Mass.: Harvard University Press, 1949), p. 28.

ship. These cannot be reconciled with the notion of independently determined desires, for their central function is to create desires —to bring into being wants that previously did not exist. This is accomplished by the producer of the goods or at his behest. A broad empirical relationship exists between what is spent on production of consumers' goods and what is spent in synthesizing the desires for that production. A new consumer product must be introduced with a suitable advertising campaign to arouse an interest in it. The path for an expansion of output must be paved by a suitable expansion in the advertising budget. Outlays for the manufacturing of a product are not more important in the strategy of modern business enterprise than outlays for the manufacturing of demand for the product. None of this is novel. All would be regarded as elementary by the most retarded student in the nation's most primitive school of business administration. The cost of this want formation is formidable. In 1956 total advertising expenditure—though, as noted, not all of it may be assigned to the synthesis of wants—amounted to about ten billion dollars. For some years it had been increasing at a rate in excess of a billion dollars a year. Obviously, such outlays must be integrated with the theory of consumer demand. They are too big to be ignored.

But such integration means recognizing that wants are dependent on production. It accords to the producer the function both of making the goods and of making the desires for them. It recognizes that production, not only passively through emulation, but actively through advertising and related activities, creates the wants it seeks to satisfy.

The businessman and the lay reader will be puzzled over the emphasis which I give to a seemingly obvious point. The point is indeed obvious. But it is one which, to a singular degree, economists have resisted. They have sensed, as the layman does not, the damage to established ideas which lurks in these relationships. As a result, incredibly, they have closed their eyes (and ears) to the most obtrusive of all economic phenomena, namely modern want creation.

This is not to say that the evidence affirming the dependence of wants on advertising has been entirely ignored. It is one reason why advertising has so long been regarded with such uneasiness by economists. Here is something which cannot be accommodated easily to existing theory. More pervious scholars have speculated on the urgency of desires which are so obviously the fruit of such expensively contrived campaigns for popular attention. Is a new breakfast cereal or detergent so much wanted if so much must be spent to compel in the consumer the sense of want? But there has been little tendency to go on to examine the implications of this for the theory of consumer demand and even less for the importance of production and productive efficiency. These have remained sacrosanct. More often the uneasiness has been manifested in a general disapproval of advertising and advertising men, leading to the occasional suggestion that they shouldn't exist. Such suggestions have usually been ill received.

And so the notion of independently determined wants still survives. In the face of all the forces of modern salesmanship it still rules, almost undefiled, in the textbooks. And it still remains the economist's mission—and on few matters is the pedagogy so firm—to seek unquestioningly the means for filling these wants. This being so, production remains of prime urgency. We have here, perhaps, the ultimate triumph of the conventional wisdom in its resistance to the evidence of the eyes. To equal it one must imagine a humanitarian who was long ago persuaded of the grievous shortage of hospital facilities in the town. He continues to importune the passers-by for money for more beds and refuses to notice that the town doctor is deftly knocking over pedestrians with his car to keep up the occupancy.

And in unraveling the complex we should always be careful not to overlook the obvious. The fact that wants can be synthesized by advertising, catalyzed by salesmanship, and shaped by the discreet manipulations of the persuaders shows that they are not very urgent. A man who is hungry need never be told of his need for food. If he is inspired by his appetite, he is immune to the influence of Messrs. Batten, Barton, Durstine & Osborn. The latter are effective only with those who are so far removed from physical want that they do not already know what they want. In this state alone men are open to persuasion.

The general conclusion of these pages is of such importance for this essay that it had perhaps best be put with some formality. As a society becomes increasingly affluent, wants are increasingly created by the process by which they are satisfied. This may operate passively. Increases in consumption, the counterpart of increases in production, act by suggestion or emulation to create wants. Or producers may proceed actively to create wants through advertising and salesmanship. Wants thus come to depend on output. In technical terms it can no longer be assumed that welfare is greater at an all-round higher level of production than at a lower one. It may be the same. The higher level of production has, merely, a higher level of want creation necessitating a higher level of want satisfaction. There will be frequent occasion to refer to the way wants depend on the process by which they are satisfied. It will be convenient to call it the Dependence Effect.

We may now contemplate briefly the conclusions to which this analysis has brought us.

Plainly the theory of consumer demand is a peculiarly treacherous friend of the present goals of economics. At first glance it seems to defend the continuing urgency of production and our preoccupation with it as a goal. The economist does not enter into the dubious moral arguments about the importance or virtue of the wants to be satisfied. He doesn't pretend to compare mental states of the same or different people at different times and to suggest that one is less urgent than another. The desire is there. That for him is sufficient. He sets about in a workmanlike way to satisfy desire, and accordingly he sets the proper store by the production that does. Like woman's his work is never done.

But this rationalization, handsomely though it seems to serve, turns destructively on those who advance it once it is conceded that wants are themselves both passively and deliberately the fruits of the process by which they are satisfied. Then the production of goods satisfies the wants that the consumption of these goods creates or that the producers of goods synthesize. Production induces more wants and the need for more production. So far, in a major *tour de force*, the implications have been ignored. But this obviously is a perilous solution. It cannot long survive discussion.

Among the many models of the good society no one has urged the squirrel wheel. Moreover, the wheel is not one that revolves with perfect smoothness. Aside from its dubious cultural charm, there are serious structural weaknesses which may one day embarrass us. For the moment, however, it is sufficient to reflect on the difficult terrain which we are traversing. We find our concern for goods undermined. It does not arise in spontaneous consumer need. Rather, the dependence effect means that it grows out of the process of production itself. If production is to increase, the wants must be effectively contrived. In the absence of the contrivance the increase would not occur. This is not true of all goods, but that it is true of a substantial part is sufficient. It means that since the demand for this part would not exist, were it not contrived, its utility or urgency, ex contrivance, is zero. If we regard this production as marginal, we may say that the marginal utility of present aggregate output, ex advertising and salesmanship, is zero. Clearly the attitudes and values which make production the central achievement of our society have some exceptionally twisted roots. . . .

THE THEORY OF SOCIAL BALANCE

The final problem of the productive society is what it produces. This manifests itself in an implacable tendency to provide an opulent supply of some things and a niggardly yield of others. This disparity carries to the point where it is a cause of social discomfort and social unhealth. The line which divides our area of wealth from our area of poverty is roughly that which divides privately produced and marketed goods and services from publicly rendered services. Our wealth in the first is not only in startling contrast with the meagerness of the latter, but our wealth in privately produced goods is, to a marked degree, the cause of crisis in the supply of public services. For we have failed to see the importance, indeed the urgent need, of maintaining a balance between the two.

This disparity between our flow of private and public goods and services is no matter of subjective judgment. On the contrary, it is the source of the most extensive comment which only stops short of the direct contrast being made here. In the years following World War II, the papers of any major city—those of New York were an excellent example—told daily of the shortages and shortcomings in the elementary municipal and metropolitan services. The schools were old and overcrowded. The police force was under strength and underpaid. The parks and playgrounds were insufficient. Streets and empty lots were filthy, and the sanitation staff was underequipped and in need of men. Access to the city by those who work there was uncertain and painful and becoming more so. Internal transportation was overcrowded, unhealthful, and dirty. So was the air. Parking on the streets had to be prohibited, and there was no space elsewhere. These deficiencies were not in new and novel services but in old and established ones. Cities have long swept their streets, helped their people move around, educated them, kept order, and provided horse rails for vehicles which sought to pause. That their residents should have a nontoxic supply of air suggests no revolutionary dalliance with socialism.

The discussion of this public poverty competed, on the whole successfully, with the stories of ever-increasing opulence in privately produced goods. The Gross National Product was rising. So were retail sales. So was personal income. Labor productivity had also advanced. The automobiles that could not be parked were being produced at an expanded rate. The children, though without schools, subject in the playgrounds to the affectionate interest of adults with odd tastes, and disposed to increasingly imaginative forms of delinquency, were admirably equipped with television sets. We had difficulty finding storage space for the great surpluses of food despite a national disposition to obesity. Food was grown and packaged under private auspices. The care and refreshment of the mind, in contrast with the stomach, was principally in the public domain. Our colleges and universities were severely overcrowded and underprovided, and the same was true of the mental hospitals.

The contrast was and remains evident not alone to those who read. The family which takes its mauve and cerise, air-conditioned, power-steered, and power-braked automobile out for a tour passes through cities that are badly paved, made hideous by litter, blighted buildings, billboards, and posts for wires that should long since have been put underground. They pass on into a countryside that has been rendered largely invisible by commercial art. (The goods which the latter advertises have an absolute priority in our value system. Such aesthetic considerations as a view of the countryside accordingly come second. On such matters we are consistent.) They picnic on exquisitely packaged food from a portable icebox by a polluted stream and go on to spend the night at a park which is a menace to public health and morals. Just before dozing off on an air mattress, beneath a nylon tent, amid the stench of decaying refuse, they may reflect vaguely on the curious unevenness of their blessings. Is this, indeed, the American genius?

In the production of goods within the private economy it has long been recognized that a tolerably close relationship must be maintained between the production of various kinds of products. Just as there must be balance in what a community produces, so there must also be balance in what the community consumes. An increase in the use of one product creates, ineluctably, a requirement for others. If we are to consume more automobiles, we must have more gasoline. There must be more insurance as well as more space on which to operate them. Beyond a certain point more and better food appears to mean increased need for medical services. This is the certain result of the increased consumption of tobacco and alcohol. More vacations require more hotels and more fishing rods. And so forth. With rare exceptions—shortages of doctors are an exception which suggests the rule—this balance is also maintained quite effortlessly so far as goods for private sale and consumption are concerned. The price system plus a rounded condition of opulence is again the agency.

However, the relationships we are here discussing are not confined to the private economy. They operate comprehensively over the whole span of private and public services. As surely as an increase in the output of automobiles puts new demands on the steel industry so, also, it places new demands on public services. Similarly, every increase in the consumption of private goods will normally mean some facilitating or protective step by the state. In all cases if these services are not forthcoming, the consequences will be in some degree ill. It will be convenient to have a term which suggests a satisfactory relationship between the supply of privately produced goods and services and those of the state, and we may call it social balance.

The problem of social balance is ubiquitous, and frequently it is obtrusive. As noted, an increase in the consumption of automobiles requires a facilitating supply of streets, highways, traffic control, and parking space. The protective services of the police and the highway patrols must also be available, as must those of the hospitals. Although the need for balance here is extraordinarily clear, our use of privately produced vehicles has, on occasion, got far out of line with the supply of the related public services. The result has been hideous road congestion, an annual massacre of impressive proportions, and chronic colitis in the cities. As on the ground, so also in the air. Planes collide with disquieting consequences for those within when the public provision for air traffic control fails to keep pace with private use of the airways.

But the auto and the airplane, versus the space to use them, are merely an exceptionally visible example of a requirement that is pervasive. The more goods people procure, the more packages they discard and the more trash that must be carried away. If the appropriate sanitation services are not provided, the counterpart of increasing opulence will be deepening filth. The greater the wealth the thicker will be the dirt. This indubitably describes a tendency of our time. As more goods are produced and owned, the greater are the opportunities for fraud and the more property that must be protected. If the provision of public law enforcement services does not keep pace, the counterpart of increased well-being will, we may be certain, be increased crime.

The city of Los Angeles, in modern times, is a near-classic study in the problem of social balance. Magnificently efficient factories and oil refineries, a lavish supply of automobiles, a vast consumption of handsomely packaged products, coupled with the absence of a municipal trash collection service which forced the use of home incinerators, made the air nearly unbreathable for an appreciable part of each year. Air pollution could be controlled only by a complex and highly developed set of public services—by better knowledge stemming from more research, better policing, a municipal trash collection service, and possibly the assertion of the priority of clean air over the production of goods. These were long in coming. The agony of a city without usable air was the result. . . .

The case for social balance has, so far, been put negatively. Failure to keep public services in minimal relation to private production and use of goods is a cause of social disorder or impairs economic performance. The matter may now be put affirmatively. By failing to exploit the opportunity to expand public production we are missing opportunities for enjoyment which otherwise we might have had. Presumably a community can be as well rewarded by buying better schools or better parks as by buying bigger automobiles. By concentrating on the latter rather than the former it is failing to maximize its satisfactions. As with schools in the community, so with public services over the country at large. It is scarcely sensible that we should satisfy our wants in private goods with reckless abundance, while in the case of public goods, on the evidence of the eye, we practice extreme self-denial. So, far from systematically exploiting the opportunities to derive use and pleasure from these services, we do not supply what would keep us out of trouble.

The conventional wisdom holds that the community, large or small, makes a decision as to how much it will devote to its public services. This decision is arrived at by democratic process. Subject to the imperfections and uncertainties of democracy, people decide how much of their private income and goods they will surrender in order to have public services of which they are in greater need. Thus there is a balance, however rough, in the enjoyments to be had from private goods and services and those rendered by public authority.

It will be obvious, however, that this view depends on the notion of independently determined consumer wants. In such a world one could with some reason defend the doctrine that the consumer, as a voter, makes an independent choice between public and private goods. But given the dependence effect—given that consumer wants are created by the process by which they are satisfied—the consumer makes no such choice. He is subject to the forces of advertising and emulation by which production creates its own demand. Advertising operates exclusively, and emulation mainly, on behalf of privately produced goods and services.[7] Since management and emulative effects operate on behalf of private production, public services will have an inherent tendency to lag behind. Automobile demand which is expensively synthesized will inevitably have a much larger claim on income than parks or public health or even roads where no such influence operates. The engines of mass communication, in their highest state of development, assail the eyes and ears of the community on behalf of more beer but not of more schools. Even in the conventional wisdom it will scarcely be contended that this leads to an equal choice between the two.

7. Emulation does operate between communities. A new school or a new highway in one community does exert pressure on others to remain abreast. However, as compared with the pervasive effects of emulation in extending the demand for privately produced consumer's goods there will be agreement, I think, that this intercommunity effect is probably small.

The competition is especially unequal for new products and services. Every corner of the public psyche is canvassed by some of the nation's most talented citizens to see if the desire for some merchantable product can be cultivated. No similar process operates on behalf of the nonmerchantable services of the state. Indeed, while we take the cultivation of new private wants for granted we would be measurably shocked to see it applied to public services. The scientist or engineer or advertising man who devotes himself to developing a new carburetor, cleanser, or depilatory for which the public recognizes no need and will feel none until an advertising campaign arouses it, is one of the valued members of our society. A politician or a public servant who dreams up a new public service is a wastrel. Few public offenses are more reprehensible.

So much for the influences which operate on the decision between public and private production. The calm decision between public and private consumption pictured by the conventional wisdom is, in fact, a remarkable example of the error which arises from viewing social behavior out of context. The inherent tendency will always be for public services to fall behind private production. . . .

THE REDRESS OF BALANCE

Our next task is to find a way of obtaining and then of maintaining a balance in the great flow of goods and services with which our wealth each year rewards us. In particular, we must find a way to remedy the poverty which afflicts us in public services and which is in such increasingly bizarre contrast with our affluence in private goods.

The problem will not be settled by a resolve to spend more for schools and streets and other services and to tax accordingly. Such decisions are made every day, and they do not come to grips with the causes of the imbalance. These lie much deeper. The most important difference between private and public goods and services is a technical one. The first lend themselves to being sold to individuals. The second do not. In the evolution of economic enterprise, the things which could be produced and sold for a price were taken over by private producers. Those that could not, but which were in the end no less urgent for that reason, remained with the state. Bread and steel went naturally to private enterprise, for they could readily be produced and marketed by individuals to individuals. Police protection, sanitation, and sewer systems remained with public authority for, on the whole, they could not. Once the decision was taken to make education universal and compulsory, it ceased to be a marketable commodity. With the rise of the national state so did national defense. The line between public and private activity, as we view it at any given moment, is the product of many forces—tradition, ideological preference, and social urgency all play some part. But to a far greater degree than is commonly supposed, functions accrue to the state because, as a purely technical matter, there is no alternative to public management.

The goods and services which are marketable at a price have a position of elementary strategic advantage in the economy. Their price provides the income which commands labor, capital, and raw materials for production. This is inherent in the productive process. In the absence of social intervention, private production will monopolize all resources. Only as something is done about it will resources become available for public services.

The solution is a system of taxation which automatically makes a pro rata share of increasing income available to public authority for public purposes. The task of public authority, like that of private individuals, will be to distribute this increase in accordance with relative need. Schools and roads will then no longer be at a disadvantage as compared with automobiles and television sets in having to prove absolute justification.

However, even though the higher urgency of the services for social balance is conceded, there is still the problem of providing the revenue. And since it is income taxes that must be used, the question of social balance can easily be lost sight of in the reopened argument over equality. The truce will be broken and liberals and conservatives will join battle on this issue and forget about the poverty in the public services that awaits correction and the poverty of people which can only be corrected at increased public cost. All this—schools, hospitals, even the scientific research on which increased production depends—must wait while we debate the ancient and unresolvable question of whether the rich are too rich.

The only hope—and in the nature of things it rests primarily with liberals—is to separate the issue of equality from that of social balance. The second is by far the more important question.

The rational liberal, in the future, will resist tax reduction, even that which ostensibly favors the poor, if it is at the price of social balance. . . .

One final observation may be made. There will be question as to what is the test of balance—at what point may we conclude that balance has been achieved in the satisfaction of private and public needs. The answer is that no test can be applied, for none exists. The traditional formulation is that the satisfaction returned to the community from a marginal increment of resources devoted to public purposes should be equal to the satisfaction of the same increment in private employment. These are incommensurate, partly because different people are involved, and partly because it makes the cardinal error of comparing satisfaction of wants that are synthesized with those that are not.

But a precise equilibrium is not very important. For another mark of an affluent society is the opportunity for the existence of a considerable margin for error on such matters. The present imbalance is clear, as are the forces and ideas which give the priority to private as compared with public goods. This being so, the direction in which we move to correct matters is utterly plain. We can also assume, given the power of the forces that have operated to accord a priority to private goods, that the distance to be traversed is considerable. When we arrive, the opulence of our private consumption will no longer be in contrast with the poverty of our schools, the unloveliness and congestion of our cities, our inability to get to work without struggle, and the social disorder that is associated with imbalance. But the precise point of balance will never be defined. This will be of comfort only to those who believe that any failure of definition can be made to score decisively against a larger idea.

The *Non Sequitur* of the "Dependence Effect"

F. A. HAYEK

Friedrich A. Hayek is Professor of Economics at the University of Freiburg. In such books as The Road to Serfdom *and* The Constitution of Liberty *he examines the economic and political conditions for a free society.*

FOR WELL over a hundred years the critics of the free enterprise system have resorted to the argument that if production were only organized rationally, there would be no economic problem. Rather than face the problem which scarcity creates, socialist reformers have tended to deny that scarcity existed. Ever since the Saint-Simonians their contention has been that the problem of production has been solved and only the problem of distribution remains. However absurd this contention must appear to us with respect to the time when it was first advanced, it still has some persuasive power when repeated with reference to the present.

The latest form of this old contention is expounded in *The Affluent Society* by Professor J. K. Galbraith. He attempts to demonstrate that in our affluent society the important private needs are already satisfied and the urgent need is therefore no longer a further expansion of the output of commodities but an increase of those services which are supplied (and presumably can be supplied only) by government. Though this book has been extensively discussed since its publication in 1958, its central thesis still requires some further examination.

I believe the author would agree that his argument turns upon the "Dependence Effect" explained in [the article which precedes this one]. The argument starts from the assertion that a great part of the wants which are still unsatisfied in modern society are not wants which would be experienced spontaneously by the individual if left to himself, but are wants which are created by

37

the process by which they are satisfied. It is then represented as self-evident that for this reason such wants cannot be urgent or important. This crucial conclusion appears to be a complete *non sequitur* and it would seem that with it the whole argument of the book collapses.

The first part of the argument is of course perfectly true: we would not desire any of the amenities of civilization—or even of the most primitive culture—if we did not live in a society in which others provide them. The innate wants are probably confined to food, shelter, and sex. All the rest we learn to desire because we see others enjoying various things. To say that a desire is not important because it is not innate is to say that the whole cultural achievement of man is not important.

The cultural origin of practically all the needs of civilized life must of course not be confused with the fact that there are some desires which aim, not at a satisfaction derived directly from the use of an object, but only from the status which its consumption is expected to confer. In a passage which Professor Galbraith quotes, Lord Keynes seems to treat the latter sort of Veblenesque conspicuous consumption [1] as the only alternative "to those needs which are absolute in the sense that we feel them whatever the situation of our fellow human beings may be." If the latter phrase is interpreted to exclude all the needs for goods which are felt only because these goods are known to be produced, these two Keynesian classes describe of course only extreme types of wants, but disregard the overwhelming majority of goods on which civilized life rests. Very few needs indeed are "absolute" in the sense that they are independent of social environment or of the

1. [Hayek is referring here to Thorstein Veblen (1857–1929), the American economist and social critic, who maintained that the "conspicuous consumption of valuable goods" was the principal means by which social standing could be enhanced. "The quasi-peaceable gentleman of leisure not only consumes of the staff of life but his consumption undergoes a specialization as regards the quality of goods consumed. He consumes freely, and of the best, in food, drink, narcotics, shelter, services, ornaments, apparel, weapons, and accoutrements, amusements, amulets, and idols of divinities. . . . Since the consumption of these more excellent goods is an evidence of wealth, it becomes honorific; and conversely the failure to consume in due quantity and quality becomes a mark of inferiority and demerit" (*The Theory of the Leisure Class*, Modern Library Edition, 1934, pp. 73–74). *Editor.*]

example of others, and that their satisfaction is an indispensable condition for the preservation of the individual or of the species. Most needs which make us act are needs for things which only civilization teaches us exist at all, and these things are wanted by us because they produce feelings or emotions which we would not know if it were not for our cultural inheritance. Are not in this sense probably all our esthetic feelings "acquired tastes"?

How complete a *non sequitur* Professor Galbraith's conclusion represents is seen most clearly if we apply the argument to any product of the arts, be it music, painting, or literature. If the fact that people would not feel the need for something if it were not produced did prove that such products are of small value, all those highest products of human endeavor would be of small value. Professor Galbraith's argument could be easily employed, without any change of the essential terms, to demonstrate the worthlessness of literature or any other form of art. Surely an individual's want for literature is not original with himself in the sense that he would experience it if literature were not produced. Does this then mean that the production of literature cannot be defended as satisfying a want because it is only the production which provokes the demand? In this, as in the case of all cultural needs, it is unquestionably, in Professor Galbraith's words, "the process of satisfying the wants that creates the wants." There have never been "independently determined desires for" literature before literature has been produced and books certainly do not serve the "simple mode of enjoyment which requires no previous conditioning of the consumer." Clearly my taste for the novels of Jane Austen or Anthony Trollope or C. P. Snow is not "original with myself." But is it not rather absurd to conclude from this that it is less important than, say, the need for education? Public education indeed seems to regard it as one of its tasks to instill a taste for literature in the young and even employs producers of literature for that purpose. Is this want creation by the producer reprehensible? Or does the fact that some of the pupils may possess a taste for poetry only because of the efforts of their teachers prove that since "it does not arise in spontaneous consumer need and the demand would not exist were it not contrived, its utility or urgency, ex contrivance, is zero"?

The appearance that the conclusions follow from the admitted facts is made possible by an obscurity of the wording of the argument with respect to which it is difficult to know whether the author is himself the victim of a confusion or whether he skilfully uses ambiguous terms to make the conclusion appear plausible. The obscurity concerns the implied assertion that the wants of consumers are determined by the producers. Professor Galbraith avoids in this connection any terms as crude and definite as "determine." The expressions he employs, such as that wants are "dependent on" or the "fruits of" production, or that "production creates the wants" do, of course, suggest determination but avoid saying so in plain terms. After what has already been said it is of course obvious that the knowledge of what is being produced is one of the many factors on which depends what people will want. It would scarcely be an exaggeration to say that contemporary man, in all fields where he has not yet formed firm habits, tends to find out what he wants by looking at what his neighbours do and at various displays of goods (physical or in catalogues or advertisements) and then choosing what he likes best.

In this sense the tastes of man, as is also true of his opinions and beliefs and indeed much of his personality, are shaped in a great measure by his cultural environment. But though in some contexts it would perhaps be legitimate to express this by a phrase like "production creates the wants," the circumstances mentioned would clearly not justify the contention that particular producers can deliberately determine the wants of particular consumers. The efforts of all producers will certainly be directed towards that end; but how far any individual producer will succeed will depend not only on what he does but also on what the others do and on a great many other influences operating upon the consumer. The joint but unco-ordinated efforts of the producers merely create one element of the environment by which the wants of the consumers are shaped. It is because each individual producer thinks that the consumers can be persuaded to like his products that he endeavours to influence them. But though this effort is part of the influences which shape consumers' tastes, no producer can in any real sense "determine" them. This, however, is clearly implied in such statements as that wants are "both passively and deliberately the fruits of the process by which they are satisfied." If the producer could in fact deliberately determine what the consumers will want, Professor Galbraith's conclusions would have some validity. But though this is skilfully suggested, it is nowhere made credible, and could hardly be made credible because it is not true. Though the range of choice open to the consumers is the joint result of, among other things, the efforts of all producers who vie with each other in making their respective products appear more attractive than those of their competitors, every particular consumer still has the choice between all those different offers.

A fuller examination of this process would, of course, have to consider how, after the efforts of some producers have actually swayed some consumers, it becomes the example of the various consumers thus persuaded which will influence the remaining consumers. This can be mentioned here only to emphasize that even if each consumer were exposed to pressure of only one producer, the harmful effects which are apprehended from this would soon be offset by the much more powerful example of his fellows. It is of course fashionable to treat this influence of the example of others (or, what comes to the same thing, the learning from the experience made by others) as if it all amounted to an attempt at keeping up with the Joneses and for that reason was to be regarded as detrimental. It seems to me not only that the importance of this factor is usually greatly exaggerated but also that it is not really relevant to Professor Galbraith's main thesis. But it might be worthwhile briefly to ask what, assuming that some expenditure were actually determined solely by a desire of keeping up with the Joneses, that would really prove?

At least in Europe we used to be familiar with a type of persons who often denied themselves even enough food in order to maintain an appearance of respectability or gentility in dress and style of life. We may regard this as a misguided effort, but surely it would not prove that the income of such persons was larger than they knew how to use wisely. That the appearance of success, or wealth, may to some people seem more important than many other needs, does in no way prove that the needs they sacrifice to the former are unimportant. In the same way, even though people are often persuaded to spend unwisely, this surely is no evidence that they do not still have important unsatisfied needs.

Professor Galbraith's attempt to give an apparent scientific proof for the contention that the need for the production of more commodities has greatly decreased seems to me to have broken down completely. With it goes the claim to have produced a valid argument which justifies the use of coercion to make people employ their income for those purposes of which he approves. It is not to be denied that there is some originality in this latest version of the old socialist argument. For over a hundred years we have been exhorted to embrace socialism because it would give us more goods. Since it has so lamentably failed to achieve this where it has been tried, we are now urged to adopt it because more goods after all are not important. The aim is still progressively to increase the share of the resources whose use is determined by political authority and the coercion of any dissenting minority. It is not surprising, therefore, that Professor Galbraith's thesis has been most enthusiastically received by the intellectuals of the British Labour Party where his influence bids fair to displace that of the late Lord Keynes. It is more curious that in this country it is not recognized as an outright socialist argument and often seems to appeal to people on the opposite end of the political spectrum. But this is probably only another instance of the familiar fact that on these matters the extremes frequently meet.

Public versus Private: Could Galbraith Be Wrong?

HENRY C. WALLICH

Henry C. Wallich is Professor of Economics at Yale University. His book The Cost of Freedom, *from which a part of this essay is taken, argues that we must not ask maximum efficiency of our economic system if we also value individual freedom.*

IN ADDITION to free advice about growth, the nation has received helpful suggestions of another sort, in a rather opposite vein. It has been argued that we have all the production we need and to spare, but that too much of our growth has gone into private consumption, too little into public. We are said to be wasting our substance on trivia while allowing urgent public needs to go uncared for. This view does not complain of inadequate growth. But it sees us riding in tail-finned, oversized automobiles through cities that are becoming slums, finds our children sitting glued to the latest TV models but lacking schools where they can learn to read properly, and generally charges us with putting private profligacy ahead of public provision.

The general doctrine that in the United States public needs tend to be underfinanced in relation to private I first heard many years ago from my old teacher Alvin Hansen. It has always seemed to me to possess a measure of appeal. Throughout this book, I have been at pains to argue that with rising wealth and industrialized living, the need for public services advances, and probably faster than living standards. In part this reflects simply the familiar fact that the demand for services tends to expand faster than the demand for goods. In part, the social conditions of modern life are also accountable for the growing need for government services. Private business is learning to meet many of these new needs—for instance in the field of insurance. It is not inconceivable that some day we shall become rich enough to be able to indulge increasingly a preference for privately supplied services. But at present, and as far ahead as one can see, the trend seems the other way. I would footnote this reference by observing that to recognize a rising trend in the need for public services and to claim that at present we have too little of them, are two different things. The more than doubling of federal and also of state and local expenditures since 1950 should drive home that distinction.

The thesis that public services are neglected and private consumption inflated with trivia has found its most eloquent interpretation in *The Affluent Society* by John Kenneth Galbraith, to whom we were previously indebted for important insights into the workings of American capitalism. Galbraith argues that this imbalance is nourished by advertising, which creates artificial wants. He sees it further accentuated by an obsession with production, which keeps us from realizing that our problems are not those of want, but of affluence. The imbalance is epitomized by our supposed tendency to limit public expenditures to what is strictly essential, while we apply no such criterion to private expenditures.

TOO MANY TRIVIA?

One may reasonably argue that Galbraith exaggerates the distorting influence of advertising. That would not alter the basic assumption on which his thesis rests—the assumption that there are better wants and worse wants. Scientific detachment notwithstanding, I find it extraordinarily difficult to disagree with this proposition. To rate an attendance at the opera and a visit to an (inexpensive) nightclub as equivalents, because the market puts a similar price on them, goes against my grain. So does the equation of a dollar's worth of education and a dollar's worth of chromium on an automobile. And a plausible case would probably be made, on the basis of the evolution of the species, that opera and education do represent more advanced forms of consumption.

But what consequences, if any, should be drawn from such judgment? It is one thing to be irritated by certain manifestations of our contemporary civilization—the gadgets, the chrome, the

tail fins and the activities that go with them. It is quite another—
and something of a *non sequitur*—to conclude from this that the
only alternative to foolish private spending is public spending.
Better private spending is just as much of a possibility.

And does this judgment yield a basis for trying to discourage
the growth of the less "good" expenditures? In a free society, we
obviously want to move with the utmost circumspection. It is
worth remembering that even Thorstein Veblen, who went to
some extreme in deriding the "leisure class" and its "conspicuous
consumption," did not take an altogether negative view of all
conspicuous waste. In *The Theory of the Leisure Class* he said,
"No class of society, not even the most abjectly poor, foregoes
all customary conspicuous consumption. . . . There is no class
and no country that has yielded so abjectly before the pressure
of physical want as to deny themselves all gratification of this
higher or spiritual need."

For fair appraisal of the case against trivia, we would also
want to know the approximate size of the bill that is being incurred for various frills and frivolities. Gadgets in cars and homes
have drawn the special ire of the critics. It is interesting to note,
therefore, that expenditures for all kinds of durable consumer
goods, including automobiles, run about 14 per cent of personal
consumption. The greater part of this, presumably, goes for the
essential parts of fairly essential equipment. What is left for ornaments and gadgets does not loom impressively large. After all,
not all the income in this country is spent by people for whom life
begins at $25,000. The median family income is $5,600. Would
the critics of the affluent society want to live on much less than
that?

Whatever our private feelings about the gadgetry in our life,
we probably do well not to stress them too hard. It is only too
easy for some members of a community to work themselves into
a fit of righteousness and to feel tempted to help the rest regulate
their existence. In an extreme form, and not very long ago, this
happened in the United States with the introduction of prohibition. Some of us may lean toward special taxation of luxuries,
but surely no one wants sumptuary legislation banishing from
our show windows and homes the offending contrivances. A new
puritanism directed against wasteful consumption, however un-

derstandable, would make no great contribution to an economy
that requires incentive goods to activate competition and free
markets. Neither would it be compatible with the freedom that
we value.

ENDS AND MEANS

It is the positive side of the case—the asserted need for more
public services—that must chiefly concern us. My contention
here will be that to talk in terms of "public vs. private" is to confuse the issue. More than that, it is to confuse means and ends.
The choice between public and private money is primarily a
choice of means. The sensible approach for those who are dis-
satisfied with some of the ends to which private money is being
spent, is to specify first what other ends are important and why.
Having determined the ends, the next step is to look to the means.
That is the order in which I propose to proceed here.

The critics are right in pointing out that new material needs
have been carried to the fore by social and economic evolution—
even though they mislabel them as public needs. In the good old
days, when this was still a nation of farmers, most people had no
serious retirement worries, there was no industrial unemployment
problem, good jobs could be had without a college degree, most
diseases were still incurable—in short, social security, education,
and health care found primitive and natural solutions within the
family and among the resources of the neighborhood. Today,
these solutions are neither adequate nor usually even possible.

Mounting wealth and advancing technology have brought
within reach the means of meeting these needs. We can afford
to live better in every way—more creature comforts, more leisure,
more attention to matters of the mind and spirit. At the same time
we can take better care of retirement, of unemployment, of ill-
ness, of education, of the possibilities opened by research, than
ever before.

There are indeed new needs. The citizen-taxpayer has his choice
of meeting them, as well as all his other needs, in one of two ways.
He can buy the goods or services he wants privately, for cash or
credit. Or he can buy them from the government, for taxes.

The nation as a whole pays taxes to buy public services as it pays grocery bills to buy groceries. The tax burden may be heavier for some individuals than for others. But the nation as a whole has no more reason to complain about the "burden" of taxes than about the "burden" of grocery bills—and no more reason to hope for relief.

Of the two stores, the private store today still is much the bigger. The public store is smaller, but it is growing faster.

Each store has some exclusive items. The private store sells most of the necessities and all of the luxuries of life, and in most of these has no competition from the government side. The public store has some specialties of its own: defense, public order and justice, and numerous local services that the private organization has not found profitable. But there is a wide range of items featured by both stores: provision for old age, health services, education, housing, development of natural resources.

THE NEW NEEDS

The bulk of the new needs are in this competitive area. The fashionable notion is to claim them all for the public store and to label them public needs. The statistics say otherwise. They say in fact two things: First, the supply of this group of goods and services has expanded very rapidly in recent years; and second, they are being offered, in varying degrees, both by the private and the public suppliers. Let us run down the list.

Provision for old age is predominantly private. The average American family, realizing that while old age may be a burden, it is the only known way to achieve a long life, takes care of the matter in three ways: (1) by private individual savings—home ownership, savings deposits, securities; (2) by private collective savings—life insurance, corporate pension funds; and (3) by public collective savings through social security. Statisticians report that the two collective forms are advancing faster than the individual. The increases far exceed the rise in the Gross National Product of almost 80 per cent (in current prices) over the past ten years; they do not indicate either that these needs are neglected or that they are necessarily public in character.

Education: the bulk of it is public; but a good part, particularly of higher education, is private. Total expenditures for all education have advanced in the last ten years from $9.3 billion to $24.6 billion ($19.3 billion of it public). Education's share in the national income has advanced from 3.8 per cent to 5.8 per cent. The silly story that we spend more on advertising than on education is a canard, though with its gross of over $10 billion, advertising does take a lot of money.

Health expenditures are still mainly private. At considerable expense, it is now possible to live longer and be sick less frequently or at least less dangerously. In the past, most people paid their own doctors' bills, although health care for the indigent has always been provided by public action or private philanthropy. Since the war, the proliferation of health insurance has given some form of collective but private insurance to three-quarters of our 182 million people. This has greatly reduced pressure for a national health service along British lines. For the aging, whose health-care needs stand in inverse proportion to their capacity to pay or insure, public insurance has finally been initiated and needs to be expanded. The total annual expenditure on health is estimated at over $25 billion, a little more than on education. Of this, about $6 billion is public.

So much for the allegation that the "new needs" are all public needs. Now for some further statistics on the public store, which is said to have been neglected. Some of them could make an investor in private growth stocks envious. Research expenditures (mainly for defense and atomic energy) have gone from about $1 billion to over $8 billion in the last ten years. Federal grants to the states have advanced from $2.2 billion to $7 billion during the same period. Social-security benefits rose from $1 billion to over $10 billion. All in all, public cash outlays (federal and state) advanced from $61 billion to $134 billion over ten years, 57 per cent faster than the GNP.

For those who feel about public spending the way Mark Twain felt about whiskey, these figures may still look slim. (Mark Twain thought that while too much of anything was bad, too much whiskey was barely enough.) To others, the data may suggest that the advocates of more public spending have already had their way. Could their present discontent be the result of not keeping their statistics up-to-date? In one of his recent pamphlets, Arthur M. Schlesinger, Jr., claims that the sum of the many neg-

lects he observes (including defense) could be mended by raising public expenditures by $10 to $12 billion. That is well below
the increase in public cash outlays that actually did take place
in one single fiscal year, from $118.2 billion in 1958 to $132.7 billion in 1959. In the three fiscal years 1957–59, these outlays went
up more than $31 billion, though the advance slowed down in
1960. More facts and less indignation might help to attain better
perspective.

Some parts of federal, state, and local budgets have expanded
less rapidly than those cited—in many cases fortunately. The massive buildup in defense expenditures from the late 'forties to the
'fifties has squeezed other programs. Unfortunately, on the other
hand, some programs that both political parties have favored—
including aid to education, to depressed areas, for urban renewal
—have been delayed unduly by the vicissitudes of politics. But
the figures as a whole lend little support to the thesis that politicians don't spend enough, and that the government store is not
expanding fast enough.

THE CITIZEN IN THE STORES

The two stores—private and public—work very hard these days
to capture the business of the citizen-taxpayer. Here is what he
hears as he walks into the private store:

"The principal advantage of this store," the private businessman says, "is that you can shop around and buy exactly what you
want. If I don't have it I'll order it. You, the consumer, are the
boss here. To be sure, I'm not in business for charity but for
profit. But my profit comes from giving you what you want. And
with competition as fierce as it is, you can be sure the profit won't
be excessive."

If the proprietor has been to Harvard Business School, he will
perhaps remember to add something about the invisible hand
which in a free economy causes the self-seeking of competitors
to work for the common good. He will also, even without benefit
of business school, remember to drop a word about the danger
of letting the public store across the street get too big. It might
endanger freedom.

As the citizen turns this sales talk over in his mind, several points occur to him. Without denying the broad validity of the argument, he will note that quite often he has been induced to buy things he did not really need, and possibly to neglect other, more serious needs. Snob appeal and built-in obsolescence promoted by expensive advertising don't seem to him to fit in with the notion that the consumer is king. Looking at the brand names and patents and trademarks, he wonders whether most products are produced and priced competitively instead of under monopoly conditions. The invisible hand at times seems to be invisible mainly because it is so deep in his pocket.

Bothered by these doubts, the citizen walks across the street and enters the public store.

"Let me explain to you," says the politician who runs it—with the aid of a horde of hard-working bureaucrats doing the chores. "The principles on which this store is run are known as the political process, and if you happen to be familiar with private merchandising they may seem unusual, but I assure you they work. First of all, almost everything in this store is free. We simply assess our customers a lump sum in the form of taxes. These, however, are based largely on each customer's ability to pay, rather than on what he gets from the store. We have a show of hands from the customers once a year, and the majority decides what merchandise the store is to have in stock. The majority, incidentally, also decides how much everybody, including particularly the minority, is to be assessed for taxes.

"You will observe," the politician continues, "that this store is not run for profit. It is like a co-operative, run for the welfare of the members. I myself, to be sure, am not in politics for charity, but for re-election. But that means that I must be interested in your needs, or you would not vote for me. Moreover, there are some useful things that only I can do, with the help of the political process, and in which you and every citizen have an interest. For instance, everybody ought to go to school. I can make them go. Everybody ought to have old-age insurance. I can make that compulsory too. And because I don't charge the full cost of the service, I can help even up a little the inequalities of life.

"By the way," the politician concludes, "if there is any special little thing you want, I may be able to get it for you, and of course it won't cost you a nickel."

The citizen has some fault to find with the political process too. He notes that there is not even a theoretical claim to the benefits of an invisible hand. Majority rule may produce benefits for the majority, but how about the other 49 per cent? Nor is there the discipline of competition, or the need for profits, to test economy of operation. There is no way, in the public store, of adjusting individual costs and benefits. And the promise to get him some small favor, while tempting, worries him, because he wonders what the politician may have promised to others. The political process, he is led to suspect, may be a little haphazard.

He asks himself how political decisions get to be made. Sometimes, obviously, it is not the majority that really makes a decision, but a small pressure group that is getting away with something. He will remember that—after payments for major national security and public debt interest—the largest single expenditure in the federal budget is for agriculture, and the next for veterans. He may also recall that one of the first budgetary actions of the new Administration was to increase funds for agriculture by $3 billion.

THE EXPANDING BELT

Next, the citizen might consider the paralyzing "balance-of-forces" effect that often blocks a desirable reshuffling of expenditures. The allocation of public funds reflects the bargaining power of their sponsors, inside or outside the government. A classical example was the division of funds that prevailed in the Defense Department during the late 'forties. Army, Navy, and Air Force were to share in total resources in a way that would maximize military potential. By some strange coincidence, maximum potential was always achieved by giving each service the same amount of money. It took the Korean War to break this stalemate.

What is the consequence of the balance-of-forces effect? If the proponents of one kind of expenditure want to get more money for their projects, they must concede an increase also to the advocates of others. More education means more highways, instead of less; more air power means more ground forces. To increase a budget in one direction only is as difficult as letting out one's belt only on one side. The expansion tends to go all around. What this comes down to is that politicians are not very good at setting priorities. Increases in good expenditures are burdened with a political surcharge of less good ones.

The last-ditch survival power of federal programs is a specially illuminating instance of the balance of forces. If a monument were built in Washington in memory of each major federal program that has been discontinued, the appearance of the city would not be greatly altered. In contrast, when the Edsel doesn't sell, production stops. But the government is still reclaiming land to raise more farm surpluses and training fishermen to enter an occupation that needs subsidies to keep alive. Old federal programs never die, they don't even fade away—they just go on.

The citizen will remember also the ancient and honorable practice of logrolling. The unhappy fate of the Area Development bill illustrates it admirably. As originally proposed, the bill sought to aid a limited number of industrial areas where new jobs were badly needed. It got nowhere in the Congress. Only when it was extended to a large number of areas with less urgent or quite different problems, were enough legislators brought aboard to pass it. Because of the heavy political surcharge with which it had become loaded, President Eisenhower vetoed the bill. A bill was finally enacted early this year, long after aid should have been brought to the areas that needed it.

Finally, the citizen might discover in some dark corner of his mind a nagging thought: Any particular government program may be a blessing, but could their cumulative effect be a threat to freedom? He has heard businessmen say this so often that he has almost ceased to pay attention to it. He rather resents businessmen acting the dog in the manger, trying to stop useful things from being done unless they can do them. He is irritated when he hears a man talk about freedom who obviously is thinking about profit. And yet—is there any conclusive rebuttal?

THE CITIZEN'S FAILURES

The citizen would be quite wrong, however, if he blamed the politician for the defects of the political process. The fault lies with the process, or better with the way in which the process, the politician, and the citizen interact. The citizen therefore would do well to examine some of his own reactions and attitudes.

First, when he thinks about taxes, he tends to think of them as a burden instead of as a price he pays for a service. As a body, the nation's taxpayers are like a group of neighbors who decide to establish a fire department. Because none is quite sure how much good it will do him, and because each hopes to benefit from the contribution of the rest, all are prudent in their contributions. In the end they are likely to wind up with a bucket brigade.

But when it comes to accepting benefits, the citizen-taxpayers act like a group of men who sit down at a restaurant table knowing that they will split the check evenly. In this situation everybody orders generously; it adds little to one's own share of the bill, and for the extravagance of his friends he will have to pay anyhow. What happens at the restaurant table explains—though it does not excuse—what happens at the public trough.

Finally, in his reaction to public or free services, the citizen takes a great deal for granted, and seldom thinks of the cost. Public beaches mistreated, unmetered parking space permanently occupied, veterans' adjustment benefits continued without need —as well as abuses of unemployment compensation and public assistance—are some examples. This applies also, of course, to privately offered benefits, under health insurance, for instance. The kindly nurse in the hospital—"Why don't you stay another day, dearie, it won't cost you anything, it's all paid for by Blue Cross"—makes the point.

By removing the link between costs and benefits, the political process also reduces the citizen's interest in earning money. The citizen works to live. If some of his living comes to him without working, he would be less than rational if he did not respond with a demand for shorter hours. If these public benefits increase his tax burden so that his over-all standard of living remains unchanged, the higher taxes will reduce his work incentive. Why work hard, if much of it is for the government?

THE POLITICAL DOLLAR AT A DISCOUNT

These various defects of the political process add up to an obvious conclusion: the dollar spent by even the most honest and scrupulous of politicians is not always a full-bodied dollar. It often is subject to a discount. It buys less than it should because of the attrition it suffers as it goes through the process, and so may be worth only 90 cents or 80 cents and sometimes perhaps less. The private dollar, in too many cases, may also be worth less than 100 per cent. But here each man can form his own judgment, can pick and choose or refuse altogether. In the political process, all he can do is say Yes or No once a year in November.

The discount on the public dollar may be compensated by the other advantages of government—its ability to compel, to subsidize, to do things on a big scale and at a low interest cost. Whether that is the case needs to be studied in each instance. Where these advantages do not apply, the private market will give better service than the political process. For many services, there is at least some leeway for choice between the private and public store—health and retirement, housing, research, higher education, natural-resource development. Defense, on the other hand, as well as public administration, public works of all kinds, and the great bulk of education—while perhaps made rather expensive by the political process—leave no realistic alternative to public action.

The argument I have offered is no plea to spend more or less on any particular function. It is a plea for doing whatever we do in the most effective way.

The Effects of Taxation on Work Incentives

GEORGE F. BREAK

George F. Break is Professor of Economics at the University of California, Berkeley. He was one of the panelists appearing before a Congressional subcommittee who contributed papers to the compendium Federal Tax Policy for Economic Growth and Stability.

THE POINT of view that high income-tax rates such as have prevailed in this country since World War II seriously sap the work incentives of the American people and thereby deter economic growth has been presented with great vigor and persistence. Typically the conclusion is treated as self-evident or as so reasonable, given a little thought, as to eliminate the need for direct empirical evidence. One may admire the strategy of this line of attack, but further investigation shows the forces involved in it to be largely illusory.

The first three sections of this paper are concerned with the economic factors which determine the influence on work incentives of the taxation of earned income. It will be seen that there are at least as good reasons for believing that such taxation will have a net incentive effect as there are for believing it will have a disincentive effect. In the next two sections a similar analysis is applied to income taxes on property incomes and to excise and sales taxes. Finally, the findings of a number of recent empirical studies of worker behavior are examined briefly. The results are likely to surprise those who have accepted the disincentive argument as conclusive. High income taxes, it would appear, have as yet not had any serious disincentive effects. It is true that some workers have been led to contract their efforts, but at the same time others have been induced to work both harder and longer. Whatever the merits of fiscal policies aimed at lowering income-tax rates may be, the encouragement of greater productive activity on the part of workers does not appear to be one of them.

INCENTIVE AND DISINCENTIVE EFFECTS OF INCOME TAXATION

To many taxpayers the disincentive proposition given at the beginning of this paper probably appears realistic enough. They may reason that "with tax rates as high as they are now it is not worth my while to do any extra work because the income from it after taxes is inadequate." The implication, of course, is that at lower tax rates the additional work would be undertaken. In reaching this conclusion, however, the taxpayer is likely to be thinking in terms of a given base income to which a larger reward from a given amount of extra work is added when tax rates are lowered. This argument overlooks an important fact—that lower tax rates would increase the taxpayer's base income—and at higher income levels, as empirical studies have shown, people typically want to take more leisure time rather than less. A lowering of income-tax rates, in short, exerts two opposing influences on work incentives: a stimulating one because after-tax rates of pay are higher, and a discouraging one because for a given amount of work taxpayers have more money. Conversely, an increase in tax rates, by lowering wage rates, tends on the one hand to induce greater effort because taxpayers find themselves with less money to spend, but, on the other, makes added effort less attractive by reducing the reward.

Some workers may react to higher taxes by simply tightening their belts, preferring to economize on consumer goods and services and on saving rather than on leisure time. Others may work more, thereby economizing on leisure as well as on other things. Still others may work less, illustrating the disincentive effects of tax increases. These people, it may be noted, show a marked lack of attachment to the rewards from productive activity, since they are led by a fall in earned income as a result of taxation to cut their incomes still further by reducing their efforts. Such a reaction is, of course, possible. To elevate possibilities of this sort to the rank of inevitabilities, as some of the more ardent critics of income taxation are prone to do, seems, however, more than a little extreme.

Another way of describing the effects of income taxes on work incentives is in terms of the value to the worker of the disposable income obtainable from the last unit of work he does. "Value" in this case does not refer simply to the number of dollars earned but more fundamentally to the usefulness of those dollars to the worker and his family. When tax rates rise the value received from a unit of effort is reduced since fewer dollars are brought home to the family coffers, but the usefulness of each dollar is increased since the family has fewer total dollars to spend. If, on balance, the value of the income earned by the last unit of effort decreases, the worker will tend to work less as a result of the increased tax rates; if, on the other hand, the value increases he will continue to work as much as before and may well wish to expand his supply of labor. Opposite results occur when tax rates are lowered. Again we note the existence of opposing lines of influence and the indeterminacy of the final outcome at this level of analysis.

High income taxes, then, do not necessarily have important disincentive effects. Some workers, it is true, may work less hard because of the influence of high tax rates. Others, however, may be led to increase their efforts, and a good many people may be virtually unaffected. Additional evidence is needed before any useful conclusions can be drawn. Fortunately, both theory and observation can help provide that evidence.

THE EFFECTS OF INFLEXIBLE MONETARY COMMITMENTS

Most of us have more than a nodding acquaintance with relatively fixed monetary commitments of one kind or another. Monthly payments on a home mortgage or rental to a landlord, life-insurance premiums, contributions to pension and annuity funds or to prepaid medical plans, union or professional dues, and other fixed costs of earning income, periodic payments incurred when consumer durables are bought on time, the obligation to support and educate children or to care for elderly relatives—all fall in this category. Possession of such commitments tends to make the taxpayer react to an increase in income taxes by increasing his efforts to earn income. The disincentive effect of lower take-home rates of pay is more than offset by the incentive push of a lower level of income when living expenses are not easily contracted.

High income taxes, therefore, are likely to have incentive effects on workers with large families, on young people who are setting up homes and acquiring their stock of consumer durables, and upon all who, for whatever reason, have become heavily indebted to others. A period following a rapid rise in consumer and mortgage debt, when higher taxes may well be called for because of strengthening inflationary pressures, is relatively favorable to the imposition of higher income taxes since their incentive effects will be intensified and their disincentive effects lessened by the previous growth in fixed-debt obligations. For similar reasons, a high and rising birthrate is favorable to high income taxes. On the other hand, Government policies which reduce the pressure of fixed monetary commitment on the worker, such as baby bonuses, provision for old age and retirement, for temporary periods of unemployment, or for sickness and injury tend, by themselves, to strengthen the disincentive effects of income taxation. These adverse tendencies, however, will be offset to the extent that Government benefits of this sort are closely matched by contributions on the part of the beneficiary.

A worker is also effectively committed to the maintenance of a given level of living in the face of an increase in income taxes if that level of living represents the minimum necessary for continued physical existence in his society. On the lowest income groups, therefore, income taxes may be expected to have incentive effects. At higher income levels the purely physical pressure of minimum subsistence is absent, but it may be replaced by equally effective social pressures—well-defined modes and standards of living which the workers feel they must maintain.

Fixed monetary commitments of various kinds, therefore, exist at all income levels. Together they provide an important set of factors which strengthen the incentive effects of high income taxes at the expense of the disincentive effects.

THE EFFECTS OF CHANGES IN PERSONAL EXEMPTION ALLOWANCES

A raising or lowering of personal exemption allowances has a powerful effect upon income-tax revenues because of the large proportion of income taxed at the lowest bracket rates. Such changes are also likely to affect work incentives. Unfortunately we can specify the result definitely only for those who remain in the same tax bracket both before and after personal exemptions are altered. For them the marginal rate of tax, and hence take-home rates of pay on the last units of work done as well as on any additional units that might be done, remains constant, while disposable incomes rise or fall as exemption allowances rise or fall. The sole effect on incentives, therefore, comes from the changes in disposable income, larger exemptions tending to reduce effort and smaller exemptions to increase it.

A large number of taxpayers, however, will be shifted into a different tax bracket when personal exemptions are changed. For them both marginal and average tax rates—i. e., take-home rates of pay and disposable incomes—change, and opposing influences on work incentives are again set in motion. Increased exemptions, for example, stimulate desires for more leisure time as a result of increased disposable incomes, but increased rates of pay at the margin make work more attractive. The strength of the latter effect will differ at different points on the income scale since rate changes from one tax bracket to the next are not uniform. By far the largest change, of course, occurs at the bottom of the tax scale where the rate plummets from 20 percent to zero for the income receiver who moves down out of the first bracket.

The net incentive or disincentive effect of a given change in personal exemptions, therefore, will depend upon the extent to which taxpayers are concentrated at the boundaries of the various tax brackets rather than at the centers. For those at the boundaries the effect may go either way, but those at the centers will be induced to work harder by reduced exemption allowances and to work less by greater exemptions. A relatively even distribution of taxpayers over the various tax brackets, therefore, would create the presumption that lower exemptions are favorable to work incentives and higher exemptions unfavorable. On the other hand, a significant concentration at the bracket boundaries, especially at the bottom of the lowest bracket, could easily produce exactly the opposite result.

THE TAX TREATMENT OF PROPERTY INCOMES

Another relevant issue to be taken into consideration in studying the incentive effects of any income tax is the treatment of incomes which are more or less independent of any labor services rendered by the income receiver. At given levels of yield—and this is the only important comparison to make—a general income tax which treats all types of income equally will be more favorable to work incentives than one which exempts some property incomes entirely and taxes others only partially.

As compared to the selective tax, the general one taxes certain kinds of property income more heavily but all other types of income less heavily. Since the two taxes are equally productive, taxpayers as a group have the same total disposable income in each case, but under the general tax they realize higher rates of take-home pay from the rendering of labor services. This acts as an incentive to still greater effort. The fact that this kind of tax treats some kinds of property income more severely has little or no effect on work incentives since little or no labor is involved in the creation of these incomes. On the average, therefore, the general tax is more favorable to productive activity. It has the further virtue, of course, of being more equitable since it treats all types of income the same way.

For these reasons policymakers should scrutinize closely proposals which would have the effect of narrowing the base of the individual income tax. If the incomes involved are largely of the property type, the influence of the income tax at given yields is shifted in the disincentive direction. Present provisions concerning capital gains and losses, tax-exempt bond interest, percentage depletion, certain allowable deductions (such as those for meals and the like, which to a large extent are personal consumption on the part of the taxpayer rather than costs of earning income) all tend to make the individual income tax less favorable to work incentives than it would otherwise be.

THE INCENTIVE ASPECTS OF EXCISE AND SALES TAXES

One of the traditional tenets with reference to the relative merits of different kinds of taxes is that excise and sales taxes are more favorable to work incentives than are income taxes. Let us examine this assumption for a moment.

Consider first the probable effects on work incentives of the price changes induced by sales and excise taxes. A general increase in consumer good prices, for example, makes consumers with relatively fixed money incomes worse off and thereby tends to induce more effort.

The rewards from that effort, however, have undergone a reduction in their buying power and so the effort itself is less attractive than it once was. When considering the extra work the worker finds himself both pushed toward it (by his lower real income) and repelled (by the lower real rates of pay) at the same time, and he may in the final analysis expand his labor supply, contract it, or leave it unchanged.

It is true that many consumers may fail to perceive the price changes induced by changes in excise taxes, but they are likely to be much more aware of what it costs them to maintain their accustomed standard of living and what happens to the level of their cash balances in the process. Some evidence of the effects of high prices on worker behavior is provided by a recent British investigation which found that approximately 40 percent of the workers interviewed regarded high prices as a factor which deterred their productive efforts and some 70 percent thought they were also a factor making for greater incentive.[1]

Taxpayers may, of course, do more work not in order to buy additional things but primarily to raise their level of saving. Even in this case, however, the tax-induced price increases are by no means irrelevant. The saving may be specifically earmarked for a future purchase of a taxed good or service. Unless the tax is believed to be temporary, the incentive effect is likely to be the same here as in the case of a person who works in order to consume. Even the person who saves in order to accumulate a certain amount of capital may adjust his goals upward when prices rise.

Finally, excise and sales taxation will affect work incentives in still another way. Such taxes reduce the money incomes of certain income receivers below the levels which would otherwise prevail. An excise tax on watches and clocks, for example, will lower the earning power of workers who are highly skilled in watchmaking, and these effects are likely to spread to all who do the same type of high-precision, fine-scale work. As we have already seen the incentive effects on these people may go either way. Lower income levels induce more effort, but reduced rates of pay have the reverse effect. Until we know more about the types of workers whose incomes are reduced by different kinds of sales and excise taxes and the extent to which these reductions take place, we cannot formulate a complete picture of the incentive-disincentive effects of sales and excise taxation.

1. Royal Commission on the Taxation of Profits and Income, *Second Report,* CMD 9105 (London, 1954), sec. 87.

THE EFFECTS OF LABOR MARKET RIGIDITIES

So far we have not concerned ourselves with the extent to which the worker is free to satisfy his own preferences with regard to the amount of labor services he supplies to the market. The great majority of workers, of course, must either have a full-time job or none at all. We cannot, however, count on this fact to neutralize, for such workers, the potential incentive or disincentive effects of income taxation. For one thing, their preferences may be only temporarily frustrated. Future bargaining with employers may restore the balance. In addition, workers typically have ways of changing their labor supply other than by altering the number of hours worked a week or the number of weeks worked a year. Overtime opportunities may be available and be refused or exploited more fully, other members of the family may enter or leave the labor force, proposed ages of retirement may be altered, or absenteeism on a day-to-day basis may change. These possibilities must be kept in mind in evaluating the results of empirical studies. Inflexible behavior in one area or disincentive effects in another do not necessarily imply either insensitivity or reduced incentives as far as the labor supply as a whole is concerned.

EMPIRICAL STUDIES OF WORK INCENTIVES

Since the pioneering work of Senator Paul H. Douglas [2] in this area, a number of empirical studies of the reactions of workers to changes in their rates of pay have been made. The results, to be sure, are incomplete. We still lack detailed information about the behavior of a number of important worker groups, especially independently employed professional and business people at the middle- to high-income levels, who are both strongly affected by income taxes and able to vary their labor supply more freely than wage earners or salaried personnel. Wage and salary workers, as noted in the preceding section, may vary their supply of labor in a number of different ways, and full information on these various possibilities is not always available even for groups that have been studied rather extensively. In addition, it has frequently been difficult to be certain that the behavior actually observed was due

2. Paul H. Douglas, *The Theory of Wages* (New York, 1934).

to changing pay rates rather than to other factors which also exert an influence on work incentives. Nevertheless, the evidence so far compiled warrants careful consideration because it is both extensive and consistent as to the direction in which it points.[3] For the most part it appears that income taxes exert relatively little influence on work incentives, and that when they do they induce greater effort as frequently as they deter it.

Thomas H. Sanders, for example, concluded, on the basis of an extensive postwar study of executive behavior, that—

the cases in which the evidence showed executives to be working harder were at least equal in number to those indicating less effort, and the former were more definitely recognizable as a tax influence.[4]

In addition, there was evidence that high taxes induced more wives of business executives to enter the labor force and, in general, led the executives themselves to postpone their dates of retirement from active participation in the business. Offsetting these tax incentives, however, was a tendency for some to refuse promotions and advantageous offers from other companies when the change meant greatly increased burdens and relatively little increase in net compensation. Finally, it was noted that a good deal of executive effort was being diverted into a study of tax laws and of ways of reducing tax burdens.

Another study of a small sample of 7 surgeons with incomes between $36,000 and $115,000 led the author to conclude "* * * we would judge that increased taxes have not reduced the surgeons' incentive." [5] He also noted that 4 of the 7 doctors planned, at the time of interview, to retire later than they had previously planned (before World War II) because they had been unable to accumulate sufficient capital. These reactions might be attributed to the influence of higher taxes or higher prices, or both.

It is interesting to note that in a recent British study, although over two-thirds of the male workers interviewed believed that

3. A more detailed summary of the results of studies of the United States labor market up to 1953 is included in the author's "Income Taxes, Wage Rates, and the Incentive To Supply Labor Services," *National Tax Journal*, VI (December 1953), 350–1. More recent investigations are noted in the text below.

4. Thomas H. Sanders, *Effects of Taxation on Executives* (Boston, 1951), p. 20.

5. Robert Davidson, "Income Taxes and Incentive: The Doctor's Viewpoint," *National Tax Journal*, VI (September 1953), p. 297.

as a general matter income taxes discouraged productive effort, less than one-third of them felt that taxes had affected their own personal effort adversely, and almost as many thought the effect was to induce them to work harder.[6] When workers who had turned down an opportunity to work overtime were asked why they had done so, only 5 percent or less of them cited high taxes in reply.[7] The National Coal Board, as a result of a number of studies of absenteeism in the British coal mines, concluded that "Tax considerations were * * * responsible for only one-third of 1 percent of the shifts lost." [8] The Royal Commission itself reached the general conclusion that "the levels of taxation within present limits do not inhibit or induce any significant proportion of the working population to modify their attitudes to their working behavior." [9]

These findings are the more significant since the pressure of taxation is in general greater in Britain than in the United States, the income tax starts at lower levels of income and its rate structure rises more steeply, and British workers are provided with comprehensive low cost medical and dental services which, alone, might be expected to push the influence of income taxes in the disincentive direction. In addition, a recent study shows that central government tax and expenditure programs have carried the redistribution of income further in Britain than in the United States.[10]

CONCLUSIONS

Human motivation is a complex phenomenon no matter what the area of study. People who are keenly interested in their jobs are not likely to be much deterred by even significant changes in

6. Royal Commission on the Taxation of Profits and Income, op. cit., secs. 74 and 81.
A similar result for the United States appears when we contrast Kimmel's 95 percent affirmative response to the question: "Do you believe that the higher the tax rate the less the incentive to work and save?" with the results of Sanders' study of executive behavior. Cf. Lewis H. Kimmel, *Taxes and Economic Incentives* (Washington, 1950), pp. 101–102.
7. Royal Commission on the Taxation of Profits and Income, op. cit., secs. 74 and 81.
8. Ibid, sec. 39.
9. Ibid, p. 115.
10. Allan M. Cartter, *The Redistribution of Income in Postwar Britain— A Study of the Effects of the Central Government Fiscal Program in 1948–49* (New Haven, 1955), especially pp. 91–92.

taxes. Strong personal ambitions may also push even very high income taxes into the background. Workers in a society that is alert and active and progressing rapidly may not be deterred in their efforts by taxation, whereas workers in a stagnant and disillusioned society might well be. Strong public support for what the Government is doing and a widespread belief that it is accomplishing its objectives in an efficient and honest manner may tend to impart favorable incentive aspects to taxation. Cultural and religious patterns, by imposing on the individual certain habits of thought and action, may govern his reactions to taxation of various kinds, and so on.

In spite of the complexities, we are by no means completely at sea. Careful empirical studies have been made and, incomplete as the results still are, it is encouraging to note that neither in Great Britain nor in the United States is there any convincing evidence that current high levels of taxation are seriously interfering with work incentives. There are, in fact, as indicated above, a number of good reasons for believing that considerably higher taxes could be sustained without injury to worker motivation should the need arise. Conversely, the social and economic need for strong work incentives does not, at the moment, make imperative a reduction in Government expenditures or an expansion in the role of excise and sales taxation in order to bring about a reduction in income taxes.

On State Expenditure

BERTRAND DE JOUVENEL

Bertrand de Jouvenel is a contemporary French political philos-opher. His book The Ethics of Redistribution, *in which this essay appears, is a critique of the welfare state.*

THE PRODUCTIVITY OF PRIVATE EXPENDITURE

THE CONCEPTS of income as the means to consumer-satisfaction and as a reward for productive effort are in economics comple-mentary, but they do not exhaust the reality of income. It is only if one pictures society as a kitchen-cum-hall stage set, where the actors can be seen on the one hand broiling some indistinguish-able 'stuff' which on the other hand they absorb, that we can be content with these two notions of income. But in fact, to keep to our theatrical comparison, what we took for the stage is only back-stage. True, the actors are busy producing the stuff that they are also consuming, eating, spreading upon their faces, turning into props, whatever you will; but this only in order to strut upon the stage. In other terms, consumption is not the ultimum, the final outcome of production; it also can be regarded as mere means to the real ultimum: human life.

Men's lives are surely to man as student the important phe-nomenon in society, the thing of beauty or at least of interest. Consumption is merely the means of supporting these lives. To the social philosopher interested in human beings it must seem absurd that one should be passionately interested in equalizing among these lives supplies of the 'stuff', on the ground that absorbing the stuff is the stuff of life. . . .

Gnawing the Income-Bone · The notion of income as means to consumer-satisfaction assumes two things: that consumption is *asocial* and that it is *unproductive*. It must be asocial, be pleasur-able or profitable to the income holder alone: under such condi-tions indeed there is no perceptible reason for allowing Primus more selfish satisfaction than Secundus. And it must be un-productive: why should Primus make a trip to Italy and not Secundus? Why indeed, if both are merely bent on pleasure jaunts? But should Primus be a young architect seeking to familiarize himself with Renaissance designs, surely his tour is not to be set on the same footing as the pleasure jaunt of Secundus!

The notion of income as means to consumer-enjoyment implies that the individual, his day's work done, his debt to society discharged, retires to masticate his income-bone in seclusion, a selfish gastric process, leading nowhere.

But it is not so. Living is a social process. Our individual life is not for ourselves alone. A generous spirit will render many services to society outside his professional activities. A professor's open table may be a means of education superior to his lectures, or complementary to them. Individual income, socially consumed, is a means to such services. These are not accounted as productive services, because they are free. The misleading picture of national income takes into account only services on which a commercial price is put. This is blinding us to the destruction of values which are not commercialized.

Further, the metaphor of the income-bone ignores the salient fact that consumption is to a large extent necessary outlay to bring forth productive activities.

From the scrap-heap of discarded notions let us for a moment rescue the 'iron law of wages', from which Marx derived his celebrated error that all the employer pays for is the cost of reproduction of the labourer's force. The 'iron-law' wage just allows the labourer to keep fit for his task. If we focus our attention on such a wage we may properly state that it includes no net income and that only whatever the worker in fact receives over and above such a wage can be accounted net income. Acting upon this assumption, practically all fiscal systems allow a basic deduction from income, this being exempt from taxation.

Proceeding therefrom, we may be tempted to say that for all income recipients there is the same basic need to be met, above which net income begins: and this is in fact the prevailing system. This idea of identical basic needs has been encouraged by its evident truth in the case of our lower functions, and by the consequent justifiable practice of food rationing.

But the reasoning is in fact very faulty: keeping a man physically fit and keeping him fit for diverse social duties are not identical notions. The same basic expenditure on basic needs which keeps a common labourer fit for his job will prove inadequate to keep a Treasury official fit for his specific task. Each specific task calls for 'functional expenditure', which is in fact cost of production and should not enter into net income.[1] . . . Social history teaches us that what we have of civilization was bought at an enormous cost, the *élites* from which we derive our culture having been supported by sweated masses—a subject on which Bakunin, among others, wrote most eloquent pages. Even in our day we meet the problem when we very properly concern ourselves with Asiatic or African populations. These can only progress through investment in *élites* as well as investment in machines. The present tendency is to provide such investments from foreign funds. But if western riches were unavailable, the choice would be between sweating their equivalent out of the mass of lower incomes or leaving matters as they are.

This point need not be laboured: it is clear enough that progress is linked with the existence of *élites*, the production and upkeep of which are costly, and the incomes of which could not be flattened out without great social loss.

The Treatment of Corporate Bodies Compared to That of Families · The egalitarian trend notwithstanding, it is generally agreed that men fulfilling certain functions need considerable means, and eventual amenities which fit them to render their specific services. But such expenditure is regarded in an entirely different light, depending on whether it is assumed by these men out of their incomes, or assumed for them by *ad hoc* institutions.

Here we come up against the feeling so prevalent in our day, that corporate bodies may do what individuals may not and that partakers in corporate existence may thereby enjoy privileges which would be denied them in their capacity as mere individuals.

Corporate bodies, *personae fictae*, enjoy in our day a quite fantastic preference over real people. The firm produces the goods, the family produces the people. It is puzzling that the needs of the former should be so well understood by the law-makers, and the needs of the latter so disregarded. It seems that law-makers can picture only the firm as an institution with a purpose and therefore respectable. The income recipient, on the other hand, his day's work done, is seen as going round the booths of a fair, blueing his rights to consumer-satisfaction. It

1. It is only the 'surplus' of incomes which one can reasonably think of equalizing.

is not realized that he is an entrepreneur in his own right. He marries, sets up a house, raises children and, it is to be assumed, struggles to bring himself and his family to the greatest possible degree of accomplishment. His achievement is to be recognized as useful to society in that he fits himself and his descendants for their roles as producers: in this respect it is an indirect contribution to the raising of national income. But the matter is not to be taken from that angle only: his achievement is far more than a contribution to *another* end, it is an end *per se*, it is *the* end of a 'good society' or a major part of it.

It is incomprehensible to the point of scandal that public authority should facilitate the upkeep of a tawdry picture or variety theatre, but not the upkeep of a great house, a thing of aesthetic and ethical value, out of which have come generations of the men who have made England what it is. Out of cinema takings, the wherewithal to preserve the cinema in its present state is deducted from taxable income. This is not so in the case of a home, and there is no reason for it other than the legislator's blind spot. It is not to be excused on the grounds that commercial ventures must be favoured over family ventures, the former being of such a nature that no one would embark upon them were they as ill-treated as the latter; for non-profit-making institutions enjoy even better treatment than commercial ventures. The family is such an institution; but as a natural body it is denied the advantages afforded to artificial bodies. . . .

Purposeful Expenditures the State's Privilege · The case for productive consumption is so strong that all opinions coincide on this point. If leftism is unwilling to take account of productive consumption in its treatment of personal incomes, it is not out of indifference to formative expenditure, but because this is regarded as henceforth the State's business. There is no sympathy for the father who spends vast sums on his son's education, and they are not accepted as costs deductible from taxable income, because the father need not, and some would say should not, bear this expenditure. The State will see to it that the boy gets the education, if state auditors so decide. The expense, and the decision, are to be taken out of private hands. It does not matter that personal incomes are so amputated as to become incapable of bearing constructive costs. They need not do so, and more precisely they are not meant to. Let the income recipient spare himself the trouble, thus recuperating net income to squander; the public authority will fulfil such of these individual purposes as are found worthy.

This attitude tends to turn personal incomes into a sum made up of the means of physical support plus pocket money. The citizen thereby loses a fundamental social responsibility: that of contributing in his private capacity to the advancement of his dependents and of his surroundings. He is encouraged to become something like a maintenance man. In so far as he adopts this attitude, equalization of incomes becomes justified. If surplus over mere cost of physical needs is to be spent at the races, why indeed should one have a greater surplus than the other?

While heads of families must perforce cease to provide accomplished and useful members of society, and are shorn of their power to advance society by their individual efforts, the State assumes full responsibility. How does it discharge it, and at what cost?

It does not see to everything, and, for instance, fails to build up homes which are an education in themselves. It does, however, spend a lot of money, and in the process it destroys the incomes of the upper and middle classes without building up those of the working classes.

A High Degree of Taxation in All Ranges · A thoroughgoing and consistent egalitarianism would redistribute incomes equally and let subsequent effects take their course. If, in such circumstances, a number of social accomplishments went undemanded, the conclusion would seem to follow that such accomplishments had no place in the 'society of equals'.

We noticed that redistributionists turn their backs on so simple a course and keep up, or even greatly develop from public funds, services which the 'society of equals' would not buy on a free market at anything like the costs assumed by the State.

The clipping of the upper- and middle-class incomes therefore necessitates an increase in public expenditure and in public taxation. [Yet] nothing like the sums which [seem] at first sight available from higher incomes [are] in fact capable of being redistributed, their contributions to the Treasury and to investment having to be deducted. But now a further most important deduction has to be made, in so far as the State proposes to restore out of public funds such formative expenditures as were previously borne by heads of families. Thus a father is not to be spared sufficient income to cover the cost of sending his son to Paris to study painting, but the State may pay for it. It is out of the question to lessen a family's taxation so that it may keep up a historic mansion, but a curator may well be appointed with a proper remuneration. . . .

The Destruction of Free Services · We have noticed that consumption is assumed in the prevailing doctrines to be both unproductive and asocial. We have discussed at some length the productive character of family consumption and seen that in so far as taxation makes productive expenditures difficult for the head of the family, such productive expenditures tend to be pushed on to corporate bodies or assumed by the State.

Let us now attend to the social character of individual, or family, expenditure. The modern statesman understands that engineers, chemists and other such must be trained and kept in a state of fitness, and [he] is quite eager that the State should assume the cost of such people, quite willing that the corporate bodies for whom they work should charge as costs functional facilities and amenities provided to these valuable citizens.

But the individual's value to society does not lie exclusively in the professional services he renders. It would be a sorry society in which men gave nothing to their contemporaries over and above the services for which they are rewarded and which enter into the computation of national income. That would be no society at all. Often enough one has a frightening vision of such a society, when one sees in some suburban train tired men travelling back from the day's toil to the small house in which they will shut themselves up to eat and sleep until they travel back to the factory or to the office. At those moments one treasures what is left of society: warm hospitality, leisured and far-ranging conversation, friendly advice, voluntary and unrewarded services. Culture and civilization, indeed the very existence of society, depend upon such voluntary, unrewarded activities. They are time- and resource-consuming and costly. There seems to be little awareness among us that they have entered upon a precipitous decline.

This decline goes unnoticed in our age of figures, and indeed the phenomenon is paradoxically shown in statistics as an increase. This occurs in so far as previously unrewarded services come to be salaried and are therefore dignified into 'output'.

Strangely enough, socialists, who dislike valuation by the market, have become dependent for their policies upon an intellectual technique which draws its validity entirely from the valuations of the market. Thereby services freely given have tended to be overlooked as against professional services. The consequences stretch very far: it has often been noted that a man and wife get worse treatment as such than they would as a combination of employer and housekeeper. In the field of public life, disregard of the value of free services works against the very principle of democracy.

Surely it is a most undesirable division of social labour which sets apart a class of public managers as against a mass of passive citizens who then are not truly citizens. Yet what else can happen if mere citizens are left no margin of resources to expend on public activity and at the same time come up against the competition of professionals? It is puzzling that private corporate interests should be allowed to count as legitimate costs propaganda for their special cause, while the citizen is allowed no margin of income with which to further his disinterested championship of the common weal.

The stripping of incomes goes so far that even hospitality tends to be discouraged. As a result of the State's assumption that consumption is *asocial* it tends to become so. The age of socialism turns out to be that in which men are most shut into their individual lives, most confined to their several paths.

Commercialization of Values · An important component of socialism was the ethical revolt against the sordid motivations of a commercial society, where everything, so the saying went, was done for money. It is, then, a paradoxical outcome of socialist policies that the services which were rendered without thought of reward should be on their way to disappearance, a number of these activities being turned into professions and therefore performed for a monetary reward. Only very careless thinking can represent modern society as one in which more and more things are freely given. Services which are paid for in bulk by taxation are not freely given. And how could they be, when the producers of these free services claim salaries equal or superior to those which reward services that the individual buys in the market? The only services which are truly free are those which are rendered by individuals exacting no payment for them: and these are most manifestly on the decline.

An unnoticed consequence of this development is that demand rules far more imperiously in our society of today than it did heretofore. Where there is no margin of leisure and income to enable individuals to offer free services, where all services can be offered only in so far as their performance is paid for, either by individual buyers or by the community, there is no opportunity of proffering services the want of which is not felt by a sufficient number of consumers or by the leaders of the community.

Let us take as an illustration the various investigations into working-class conditions made in the nineteenth century. Such work was at the time susceptible of being rewarded neither by the commercial market nor by the government. It is an arresting thought that the writing of Marx's *Das Kapital* was made possible only by Engels' benefactions out of untaxed profits. Marx did not have to sell his wares on the market, not did he have to get his project accepted by a public foundation of learning. His career testifies to the social utility of surplus incomes. It is of course assumed by *Etatistes* of today that Marx under the new dispensation would benefit from ample and honourable public support. But it seems so to them because his idea is now an old one and is accepted as the prevailing prejudice of our time. An innovator as bold today as he was in his day would not get by the boards of control which administer public funds. . . .

The more one considers the matter, the clearer it becomes that redistribution is in effect far less a redistribution of free income from the richer to the poorer, as we imagined, than a redistribution of power from the individual to the State.

Redistribution an Incentive to Tolerating the Growth of Public Expenditure · Public finance generally is a dull subject, but public finance in the first half of the twentieth century is entrancing: it has been revolutionized and in turn has been the means of a revolution in society. Out of many new aspects of public finance, the two most notable are, first, that it has been used to alter the distribution of the national income between social classes and, second, that the fraction of national income passing through public hands has enormously increased.

The point I propose to make here is that avowed redistributionist policies have made possible the tremendous growth of taxation and public expenditure. The role played by the State in transferring incomes evidently entailed some increase in the volume of public encashing and payments, but this volume has grown out of all proportion to the needs of this function. Such growth has encountered only the weakest opposition; my argument is that a change of mind towards public expenditure has been induced by redistributionist policies, the greatest gainer from which is not the lower-income class as against the higher but the State as against the citizen.

Let us recall that in past phases of history the public authorities have found it difficult not only to increase their fractional share of national income but also, even in a period of rising real or nominal incomes, to retain the same proportion of this income as they previously enjoyed. The revolutions which occurred in Europe between 1640 and 1650, the English Revolution, the Naples revolution, and France's abortive *Fronde,* all seem to be linked with resistance by taxpayers to government demands for more funds in view of the price relvolution. The old attitude of taxpayers was ruled by the desire to keep the government down to its usual takings in nominal terms. It is then almost incredible that, notwithstanding the period of inflation we have gone through, governments of our century should have found it possible to obtain an ever-increasing fraction of the nations' income.

Resistance to taxation has not always been general: the late Stuarts and the late Bourbons kept small groups of pensioners who were all for increasing the load of the many. It was then made one of the cardinal principles of taxation that it was to spare no one and to benefit no special group. These principles were infringed early in this century when the State began to subsidize, albeit modestly, special services for specific groups; simultaneously a new mode of taxation was adopted, surtax, which bore only upon a minority. This was the thin end of a wedge driven into the solidarity of taxpayers. When war demanded a huge increase in the rate of income-tax, this became quite unbearable for the poorer taxpayers, and deductions and allowances were necessary; these were compensated by an increasing steepness of surtax. Thus the very heaviness of taxation made necessary a difference of treatment between the different income classes. When, at the end of the war, the State retained part of its taxation gains, it excused its avidity by providing net ɀdvantages out of taxation to the unfavoured mass. Thus a great increase in state takings and expenditure was made tolerable to the majority by some measure of redistribution, and the process was repeated and enhanced during and after World War II.

It is not meant to imply that any conscious policy of breaking down taxpayer's resistance by advantages given to the poorer majority was at any time pursued by anyone. But the fact is that all the steps in the swelling of the Budget were coupled with increasing inequality of treatment, deductions, allowances and positive benefits for the citizens in the lower-income ranges.

Redistribution Incidental to Centralization? · In our exploration we have found ourselves repeatedly coming across centralization as the major implication of redistributionist policies. In so far as the State amputates higher incomes it must assume their saving and investment functions, and we come to the centralization of investment. In so far as the amputated higher incomes fail to sustain certain social activities, the State must step in, subsidize these activities, and preside over them. In so far as income becomes inadequate for the formation and expenses of those people who fulfil the more intricate or specialized social functions, the State must see to the formation and upkeep of this personnel. Thus the consequence of redistribution is to expand the State's role. And conversely, as we have just seen, the expansion of the State's takings is made acceptable only by measures of redistribution.

We then may well wonder which of these two closely linked phenomena is predominant: whether it is redistribution or centralization. We may ask ourselves whether what we are dealing with is not a political even more than a social phenomenon. This political phenomenon consists in the demolition of the class enjoying 'independent means' and in the massing of means in the hands of managers. This results in a transfer of power from individuals to officials, who tend to constitute a new ruling class as against that which is being destroyed. And there is a faint but quite perceptible trend towards immunity for this new class from some part of the fiscal measures directed at the former.

This leads the observer to wonder how far the demand for equality is directed against inequality itself and is thus a fundamental demand, and how far it is directed against a certain set of 'unequals' and is thus an unconscious move in a change of *élites*.

Why the Government Budget Is Too Small in a Democracy

ANTHONY DOWNS

Anthony Downs, political theorist and economist, is the author of An Economic Theory of Democracy. *He is at present associated with the RAND Corporation. This article appeared in the July 1960* World Politics.

IN A DEMOCRATIC society, the division of resources between the public and private sectors is roughly determined by the desires of the electorate. But because it is such a complex and time-consuming task to acquire adequate political information, the electorate is chronically ignorant of the costs and benefits of many actual and potential government policies. It is my belief that this ignorance causes governments to enact budgets smaller than the ones they would enact if the electorate possessed complete information. Yet these undersized budgets stem from rational behavior by both the government and the electorate; hence they are extremely difficult to remedy. Furthermore, the resulting misallocation of resources becomes more and more serious as the economy grows more complex.

As proof of these assertions, I shall present a model of a democratic society based upon the principles set forth in *An Economic Theory of Democracy* (New York, 1957). The basic rules for government and voter decision-making in this model are hypotheses, but the environment in which they are set resembles the real world as closely as possible. Furthermore, I believe the hypotheses themselves are accurate representations of what happens in the real world most of the time. My belief is based upon a comparison of the deductions made from these hypotheses in *An Economic Theory of Democracy* with the actual behavior of political parties in various democracies. However, the deductions made from the same hypotheses in this article are harder to compare directly with reality. Nevertheless, if the reader agrees with me that the basic hypotheses are realistic, it should follow that he will find the conclusions of this model meaningful in real-world politics as well as in the theoretical world of my argument.

This argument consists of the following topics: (1) how the budget is determined in a democracy, (2) the nature of rational political ignorance, (3) the definition of "correct" and "incorrect" budgets, (4) how an "incorrect" budget might arise, (5) significant differences between transactions in the public and private sectors, (6) distortions in budget evaluation arising from these differences, (7) a countertendency toward overexpenditure, and (8) the net results.

HOW THE BUDGET IS DETERMINED IN A DEMOCRACY

According to the economic theory of democracy, each government sets both expenditures and revenue collection so as to maximize its chances of winning the next election.[1] This follows from the axiom that political parties are primarily motivated by the desire to enjoy the income, prestige, and power of being in office. Each party regards government policies as means to these ends; hence it pursues whatever policies it believes will gain it the political support necessary to defeat its opponents. Since expenditures and taxes are two of the principal policies of government, they are set so as to maximize political support. Out of this rational calculation by the governing party comes the budget.

Rationality likewise prevails among voters. They vote for the party whose policies they believe will benefit them more than those of any other party.[2] These "benefits" need not be conceived in a narrowly selfish sense, but consist of any utility they derive from government acts, including acts which penalize them economically in order to help others.

The budget itself is not arrived at by considering over-all spending versus over-all taxation, but is the sum of a series of separate policy decisions. The governing party looks at every possible expenditure and tries to decide whether making it would gain more vote than financing it would lose. This does not mean that each spending bill is tied to a particular revenue bill. Instead all proposed expenditures are arranged in descending order of their vote-gain potential, and all proposed revenue col-

1. For a complete explanation of this theory, see *An Economic Theory of Democracy*. The government budget is discussed in Ch. 4.

2. The remainder of this article assumes a two-party system. Its conclusions are also applicable to multi-party systems, but the corresponding proofs are too complicated to be presented in an article of this length.

lections arranged in ascending order of their vote-loss potential. Wherever these two marginal vote curves cross, a line is drawn that determines the over-all budget. Expenditures with a higher vote-gain potential than the marginal one are included in the budget, which is financed by revenue collection methods with lower vote-loss potentials than the marginal one.

Because of the myriad expenditures made by modern governments, this rule may seem impractical. In the real world, it is true, the governing party does not weigh the vote impact of every single expenditure, but groups them into large categories like national defense. It then balances the marginal vote-gain of spending for each such category against its marginal vote-cost and against the marginal vote-gains of spending for other large categories, such as farm subsidies, education, and social security. Thus, in the real world, the aggregate budget for each category is decided in a manner similar to that described above, even though details of spending within the category may be left to nonpolitical administrators.[3]

It should be noted that the government in our model never asks itself whether the over-all budget is "too large" or "too small" in relation to the views of the electorate. In fact, it never makes any explicit decision about what the over-all budget size should be, but determines that size merely by adding up all the items that more than pay for themselves in votes. Similarly, the voters do not evaluate a budget on the basis of its total size but by the particular benefits and costs it passes on to them.

The absence of any specific evaluation of over-all budget size appears to make our original assertion meaningless. How can we say the government budgets are too small when no one ever considers their size in judging them? The answer is that ignorance produces biases in the electorate that cause the government to exclude certain acts from the budget, thus reducing its size

3. Some readers of this argument may object that spending for such categories as national defense cannot be evaluated in terms of votes but must be decided largely on technical grounds. I do agree. For example, the United States government chose to abandon maintenance of strong conventional forces and stake the nation's entire defense upon the use of nuclear weapons. This decision was made against the technical advice of Army planners. From statements made by leading government officials at the time, it is clear that the decision was designed primarily to avoid asking the electorate to pay for both nuclear and conventional forces. Thus in the real world, even regarding national defense, major budgetary questions are usually decided by vote possibilities.

from what it "should be." Our original thesis can be more accurately stated as follows: rational ignorance among the citizenry
leads governments to omit certain specific types of expenditures
from their budgets which would be there if citizens were not
ignorant. The fact that this results in budgets that are too small
is simply a dramatic way of stressing the outcome.

RATIONAL POLITICAL IGNORANCE

In this model, information is a crucial factor. In order to form
policies, each party must know what the citizenry wants; and in
order to vote rationally, each voter must know what policies the
government and its opponents espouse. But in the real world,
information is costly—if not in money, at least in time. It takes
time to inform yourself about government policy. Furthermore,
the number of policies that a modern government has to carry
out is vast and their nature astoundingly complex. Even if the
world's most brilliant man spent twenty-four hours a day reading
newspapers and journals, he would be unable to keep himself
well-informed about all aspects of these policies.

In addition to facing this problem, the average voter knows
that no matter how he votes, there are so many other voters that
his decision is unlikely to affect the outcome. This does not always prevent him from voting, because he realizes voting is essential to democracy and because it costs so little. But it usually
does prevent him from becoming well-informed. Beyond the free
information he picks up just by being alive in our media-
saturated world, he does not see how acquiring detailed political
data will make him better off. Thus a rationally calculating attitude about the use of time leads him to political ignorance. This
conclusion is borne out by countless polls that show just how
ignorant the average citizen is about major political questions
of the day.

In this article we discuss three specific states of rational ignorance. The first is *zero ignorance*—i.e., perfect knowledge. In this
state, citizens know (1) all actual or potential items in the
budget of each party and (2) the full benefits and costs of each
item. The second state is *partial ignorance*, in which voters know
all the actual or potential items in the budget, but not all the
benefits and costs attached to each item. Their political perception threshold has been raised so that remote or extremely com-

plex events do not cross it, though the budget itself still does. The third state is *preponderant ignorance,* in which citizens are ignorant of both the items in the budget and their benefits and costs. In this state, citizens' perception thresholds are so high that they are aware of only the individual policies or items in the budget that vitally affect them.

"CORRECT" AND "INCORRECT" BUDGETS

My contention is that rational ignorance acts so as to produce an "incorrect" government budget. But what is meant by the term "incorrect" when the government does not seek to maximize welfare? Since I posit no social-utility function, how can I say that one budget is "better" or "worse" than another except in terms of its vote-getting power? My answer is that the "correct" budget is the one which would emerge from the democratic process if both citizens and parties had perfect information about both actual and potential government policies. Insofar as an actual budget deviates from the "correct" budget, it is "incorrect." Admittedly, no one has perfect information; hence no one can say what budget would exist if there were no rational ignorance in politics. This fact prohibits use of the "correct" budget for detailed criticism of actual budgets, but it does not prevent generalizations about the tendency of actual budgets to deviate from "correct" budgets because of broad social factors like rational ignorance.

There is no point in denying that the terms "correct" and "incorrect" are ethical judgments. They presuppose that it is good for the citizens in a democracy to get what they want, and to base their wants on as much knowledge as possible. It is not good for them to get something they would not want if they knew more about it. That is the extent of my ethical foundation, and I think it is compatible with almost every normative theory of democracy.

HOW AN "INCORRECT" BUDGET MIGHT OCCUR

In a two-party democracy like ours, each national election can be considered a contest between two prospective government budgets. These budgets differ from each other in both quality and quantity, but each contains any spending and taxing measures about which there is strong majority consensus. In reality, many factors besides budgets influence people's political choices. However, most of these factors are in some way reflected in the budget, and in the rational world of economic theory we can assume that proposed budgets have a decisive role in determining how people vote. Knowing this, each party carefully plans its budget so as to maximize the support it gets, following the procedure described in the first section.

A key feature of this procedure is that the government gives voters what they want, not necessarily what benefits them. As long as citizens know what benefits them, there should be no difference between the actual budget and the "correct" budget. But if there are benefits which government spending would produce that people are not aware of, the government will not spend money to produce them unless it believes it can make them well-known before the next election. For the government is primarily interested in people's votes, not their welfare, and will not increase their welfare if doing so would cost it votes. And it would lose votes if it increased taxes or inflation—which people are aware of—in order to produce benefits which people are not aware of. Many citizens would shift their votes to some other party that produced only more tangible benefits at less total cost—even if they would in fact be worse off under this party.

Thus if voters are unaware of the potential benefits of certain types of government spending, party competition may force the actual budget to become smaller than the "correct" budget. This outcome may result even if voters merely discount certain classes of government benefits more heavily than comparable private benefits when in reality they are equal. Thus complete ignorance of benefits is not necessary to cause a "too small" budget—only relative unawareness of certain government benefits in relation to their cost, which under full employment consists of sacrificed private benefits.

Conversely, if citizens are less aware of certain private benefits than they are of government benefits, or if they see benefits more clearly than costs, the actual budget may tend to exceed the "correct" budget. In either case, ignorance causes a distorted evaluation of the relative benefits of public and private spending. This distortion is carried over into the budget by interparty competition, which forces each party to give voters what they want—

not necessarily what the parties think would benefit them. Thus the ignorance of the voters may cause the actual budget to deviate from the "correct" budget.

Whether the actual budget is too large or too small depends upon the specific forms of ignorance present in the electorate. Since ignorance influences voters' thinking by distorting their evaluation of public vs. private spending, we must study the way citizens view these two types of spending before analyzing the net impact of ignorance upon the budget.

SIGNIFICANT DIFFERENCES BETWEEN TRANSACTIONS IN THE PUBLIC AND PRIVATE SECTORS

There are two significant differences between transactions in the private sector and in the public sector that are relevant to our analysis. First, in the private sector nearly all transactions are made on a *quid pro quo* basis, whereas in the public sector benefits are usually divorced from the revenues that make them possible. Whenever a citizen receives a private benefit, he pays for it directly and individually. Conversely, whenever he pays someone in the private sector, he receives a corresponding benefit which he has freely chosen because he wants it. No such direct link between costs and benefits exists in the public sector. Taxes are not allocated to individuals on the basis of government benefits received but on some other basis, usually ability to pay. Thus receipt of a given benefit may have no connection whatever with payment for it. And when a man pays his income tax or the sales tax on his new car, he cannot link these acts of sacrifice to specific benefits received. This divorce of benefits from payment for them makes it difficult to weight the costs and benefits of a given act and decide whether or not it is worthwhile, as can be done regarding almost every private transaction.

There are two reasons why governments do not operate on a *quid pro quo* basis. First, the collective nature of many government benefits makes it technically impossible. For example, take national defense, which is the largest single item of government spending in most democracies. But the benefits of national defense are collective in nature; that is, if they exist for one man, all men enjoy them. This fact makes *quid pro quo* transactions impossible, because once the benefits exists, enjoyment of it cannot be denied to those citizens who have not paid for it. For this reason, voluntary payment cannot be used to finance collective benefits. Since each citizen benefits whether or not he has paid, he maximizes his income by dodging his share of the cost. But *everyone* has this cost-minimizing attitude; so if voluntary payment is relied upon, no one pays. Consequently the resources necessary to provide the collective good are not provided, and no one receives any benefits. To avoid this outcome, individuals agree to coerce each other into payment through a collective agency like the government.

A second reason why governments do not use *quid pro quo* transactions is their desire to redistribute income. In the private sector, benefits are furnished only to those who can pay for them, or through voluntary charitable activities. But most modern democracies have elected to provide their poorest citizens with more benefits than those citizens can afford individually. This goal requires a deliberate violation of the *quid pro quo* relationship; pool citizens get more benefits than they pay for, and their richer brethren are forced to give up more in taxes than is spent on benefits for them. One way to accomplish such redistribution and at the same time allocate the costs of collective goods is to tax on the basis of ability to pay. Thus for both technical and ethical reasons, the benefit principle that prevails in the private sector is largely abandoned in the public sector.

The second major difference between transactions in the private and public sectors is the coercive nature of dealings in the latter. Whereas all private transactions are voluntary, most payments to governments—other than direct sales of services—are enforced by law. Even the receipt of collective benefits is involuntary, since they exist whether a given citizen wants them or not. As noted, coercion is necessary because there is no intrinsic link between benefits and payments as in the private sector. Instead, force supplies this link.

But the use of force makes doing business with the government an all-or-nothing proposition. In the private sector, a citizen can enter into those transactions he desires and refrain from those he does not desire. No such selectivity is possible in his dealings with government. He must pay taxes that are used to pay for many projects he does not want. . . . The result is that no one ever attains marginal equilibrium in his dealings with the government.

For a citizen, such equilibrium exists when the utility produced by that act of government which is least attractive to him (*i.e.*, the "last" government act on his preference scale) is equal to the utility of the least attractive act he undertakes in the private sector (*i.e.*, the "last" completed private act on his preference scale). Furthermore, there must be no additional government acts that would give him more utility than those now being carried out. Under these circumstances, the individual cannot be made better off by shifting resources from the private to the public sector or vice versa, or by any reallocation of resources within the public sector. (We assume he has already allocated his resources within the private sector to his maximum benefit.) This situation corresponds to equilibrium within the private sector as portrayed by classical economists—a state attained by utility-maximizers in a world of perfect competition.

However, even if perfect competition exists, the requirements for attaining perfect equilibrium with a democratic government are highly restrictive. If a majority of citizens have identical preference rankings of both public and private acts, then the government's actual policies will be just what those citizens want (assuming the government knows what their preference rankings are). The division of resources between public and private sectors will be precisely that necessary to assure the majority a state of equilibrium between the sectors.

But, in the real world, people's preference rankings are not identical, so we shall not assume them identical in our model. While almost every man agrees with a majority of his fellows in regard to some policies, he also finds himself in a minority regarding others. It is the presence of these "revolving majorities" that prevents men from attaining equilibrium with governments. The government must carry out a complex mixture of many policies, some pleasing to one majority, some pleasing to another majority, and some pleasing only to a minority with intensive feelings concerning them. It can afford to undertake policies favored only by a minority because it does not stand or fall on any one issue but on the mixture as a whole. If society is at all complex, the government's gigantic policy mix is bound to contain at least one act which any given voter opposes. As long as only one such act exists for him, he is out of equilibrium with government. Even if we assume declining marginal utility of income in both private and public sectors, there is always some additional private use of resources (including charity) which would yield him positive utility. There may also be other government acts, not now being performed, which would yield him even more utility than the best private act he can think of. Hence his disequilibrium does not necessarily imply a desire to shift resources from the public to the private sector. It may also imply desire for reallocation within the public sector or even for moving more resources into that sector. But, in any case, there is always some change in government policy that would benefit him. Furthermore, the government is always spending money on projects he dislikes; hence his welfare would be improved if those projects were eliminated and his taxes reduced. *Therefore every citizen believes that the actual government budget is too large in relation to the benefits he himself is deriving from it.* Even if he feels the optimum budget would be much larger than the actual one, he believes the actual one could be profitably reduced "through greater economy"—*i.e.*, elimination of projects from which he does not benefit.

But if everyone feels the government is spending too much money for the benefits produced, why don't political parties propose smaller budgets? How can budgets which everyone regards as too large keep winning elections? The answer lies in the nature of the "revolving majorities" discussed previously. According to the economic theory of democracy, governments never undertake any policies unless they expect to win votes (or at least not lose votes) by doing so. Hence for every citizen opposed to a given act, there are other citizens in favor of it. Elimination of that act would please the former but alienate the latter. Looking at the whole complex of its acts between elections, the governing party feels that including this act gains more votes than excluding it. The party can afford to offend some voters with this act because they are in the minority regarding it, their feelings against it are not as intensive as the feelings of those for it, some other acts will placate them, or for some combination of these reasons. Since citizens' preferences are diverse, every man finds himself thus ignored by the government on some policy or other. Hence everyone believes the government is carrying out some unnecessary acts.

However, the resulting disequilibrium puts tremendous pressure on the government to reduce the budget wherever it can. This means it will make only those expenditures which produce benefits that voters are aware of, for hidden benefits cannot influence votes. Thus the threat of competing parties prevents the government from giving citizens what is good for them unless they can be made aware of the benefits involved before the next election. Only if a party has immense confidence in its ability to win the next election anyway is it free to produce such hidden benefits, no matter how important they are in the lives of the voters. The more "perfect" the competition between parties, the more closely must the government follow popular opinion, and the more likely it is to include in its policies any errors in that opinion caused by ignorance.

DISTORTIONS IN BUDGET EVALUATION ARISING FROM THESE DIFFERENCES

Having analyzed the relevant differences between transactions in the public and private sectors, we now turn to the distortions they produce in benefit-appraisal. Such distortions are of two main types: underevaluation of government benefits in comparison with private benefits and underevaluation of government cost in comparison with private cost. In both cases, the distortion occurs in estimating the government's contribution or cost rather than that of the private sector. This is true because the *quid pro quo* relationship in the private sector makes accurate estimation of both costs and benefits almost universal. The absence of these qualities in public transactions gives rise to two major sources of error.

Remoteness · Benefits from many government actions are remote from those who receive them, either in time, space, or comprehensibility. Economic aid to a distant nation may prevent a hostile revolution there and save millions of dollars and even the lives of American troops, but because the situation is so remote, the average citizens—living in rational political ignorance—will not realize he is benefiting at all. Almost every type of preventive action, by its nature, produces such hidden benefits. People are not impressed with their gains from water purification, regulation of food and drugs, safety control of airways, or the regulation of utility and transport prices, unless these actions fail to accomplish their ends. Then, perhaps for the first time, the absence of effective protection makes them aware of the benefits they were receiving when it was present.

In contrast, the immediate benefits of almost all private goods are heavily emphasized. In order to sell these goods on a voluntary basis, their producers must convince the public of their virtues. Thus consumers are subject to a continuous advertising barrage stressing the joys of private goods, whereas no comparable effort dramatizes the benefits they receive from government action. Even private goods with benefits of a remote nature, such as cemetery lots, are advertised in such a way as to make awareness of these benefits immediate.

Furthermore, much of the cost of remote government benefits is not equally remote. In the private sector, the *quid pro quo* balancing of costs and benefits is often attenuated by time-payment plans which magnify benefits in relation to costs. But in the public sector the opposite is true. The major source of federal government revenue—personal and corporate income taxes—must be computed by taxpayers on an annual basis. . . .

The confiscatory cast of taxation is an inevitable result of the divorce of costs from benefits and the remoteness of the latter. Whereas in *quid pro quo* transactions each yielding of resources is justified by immediate receipt of benefits, taxation appears to be outright seizure of privately produced resources. It thus seems parasitic, rather than self-supporting like other costs of production or consumption. True, a rational taxpayer knows that he receives benefits in return for his taxes, but the remoteness of many such benefits removes the appearance of tit-for-tat balance that is present in private transactions.

In summary, a major portion of government benefits is remote in character compared with either taxes or private benefits. Since citizens are rationally ignorant of remote political events, they fail to realize all the government benefits they are receiving. However, they are well aware of a greater percentage of the taxes they pay and of the private benefits they are sacrificing to pay them. Because of this imbalance, the governing party cannot spend as much money on producing remote benefits as their real value to the citizenry warrants. Every dollar raised by taxation (or inflation) costs votes which must be compensated for by votes won through spending. But when the spending produces benefits that are not appreciated by voters, no compensating votes are forthcoming. Hence such spending must be restricted, or else the competing party will gain an advantage by cutting its own (proposed) spending and charging the incumbents with "waste." True, if the incumbents can demonstrate to the voters that this spending actually produces valid benefits, such charges will be harmless. But such demonstrations absorb resources themselves, especially since the nature of remote benefits makes them hard to document. And since the government is under constant pressure to cut expenditures, it cannot afford to use resources advertising the benefits of its policies for fear of being accused of wasting public funds.

The outcome is a tendency toward elimination from the budget of all expenditures that produce hidden benefits. Only if the benefits involved are necessary for the survival of democracy itself will the governing party risk losing votes by producing them and spending resources to justify its actions. Even in this case, it tends to get by with the minimum possible amount because its fears charges of "waste" from its opponents. Clearly, this situation causes government budgets to be smaller than they would be if voters were perfectly informed about all benefits and costs, however remote.

Uncertain Nature of Government Benefits · Closely akin to remoteness is the uncertain nature of many government benefits compared with private ones. Since government must deal with factors affecting society as a whole, the problems it faces are much more complex than the problems facing individuals in their private lives. Many policies undertaken by governments are launched without either control or knowledge of exactly what their outcomes will be. This is particularly true in international relations or fields of rapid obsolescence, such as national defense. Here the future is so beset by unknowns that whether a given policy will produce benefits or penalties is often problematical, and appraisal of the expected value of benefits forthcoming is extremely difficult. In contrast, each citizen in his private life knows of many ways to invest resources which will give him immediate benefits. True, life is full of risks, and the future is unknown to individuals as well as governments. Nevertheless, each person faces a much simpler set of choices in his own life, with many fewer parameters, than does even a local government. Hence the returns from investing resources privately must be discounted much less than those from investing resources publicly.

This situation is not a result of rational political ignorance, but of the uncertainty inherent in any complex situation involving human action. Even the best-informed government experts cannot predict the outcome of many of their policies. They have plenty of current information, but do not understand all the basic forces at work, and cannot predict the free choices of the men involved. This kind of ignorance cannot be removed by greater personal investment in political information.

Again, the outcome is a budget smaller than the "correct" one. Because voters are led by rational ignorance to undervalue benefits from policies with uncertain outcomes, the government cannot count on gaining political support by spending money on these policies. But since it can count on losing support by raising the money, it tends to eschew such policies altogether.

Throughout the preceding argument, it is assumed that citizens' ignorance conceals benefits lost through failure to spend but does not conceal losses of utility through excessive spending. Perhaps if citizens became better informed about government policy, they would discover that present policies produce fewer benefits than they had supposed. In that case, increased information might increase their reluctance to transfer resources into the public sector. In other words, they would discover that the actual budget was larger than the "correct" budget instead of smaller.

This objection to our previous conclusion ignores the motivation of the government in regard to expending resources. Essentially, the argument implies that government conceals a great deal of "waste" spending under the cloak of citizens' ignorance; therefore if citizens had perfect information, they would want the government to eliminate this waste. Naturally, in a world of imperfect knowledge, every government makes mistakes, and undoubtedly perfect information would reveal such errors and cause the electorate to desire corrective reallocations. But, aside from this failing, the government has no motive to spend resources without producing tangible benefits. As we have seen, government policies are designed to gain votes by producing definite benefits known to voters. Furthermore, because voters are aware of the costs imposed upon them by government action, government is always under pressure to eliminate policies that do not justify their costs by producing tangible benefits. Hence it is irrational for government to "waste" resources on nonbenefit-producing policies, since they lose votes through adding to taxation but do not gain votes by adding to benefits. Such "waste" expenditures would be rational only if (1) the government had a secondary motive of maximizing expenditures *per se* in addition to maximizing its chances for election, or (2) in the process of winning votes, the government spent money to benefit minorities in hidden ways which the majority would repudiate if they had perfect knowledge. The first case posits a government markedly different from the one in our model. Exploration of the behavior of such a government might be very interesting, but it cannot be undertaken in this article. The second case will be dealt with in the next section.

THE TENDENCY TOWARD EXCESSIVE SPENDING

Up to this point we have discussed two states of information in the electorate: perfect knowledge and partial ignorance. We have shown that when the latter prevails, costs of government action will appear more significant than benefits; so the actual budget will be smaller than the "correct" budget. However, there is also a third state of information: preponderant ignorance. In this state, citizens are ignorant of both the items in the budget and their benefits and costs. The budget that results when such ignorance predominates differs radically from those discussed previously: it tends to be *larger* than the correct size because of voters' ignorance of what items are in the budget.

Government action affects each citizen in many ways, touching nearly all the functional "roles" he plays in society. Two important such roles are those of income-earner and consumer. As an income-earner, each citizen benefits when government spending increases the demand for the service he produces and when his taxes are reduced. He suffers when such spending is diminished or when his taxes increase. As a consumer, he suffers whenever government action increases the prices of the goods and services he buys, and he gains when it causes them to fall relative to his income.

Thus government action influences his welfare in both roles, but the two influences are not equally significant to him. Since almost every citizen receives nearly all his income from one source, any government act pertinent to that source is extremely important to him. In contrast, he spends his income on many products, each one of which absorbs a relatively small part of his total budget. Thus a government act which influences one of the products he consumes is nowhere near as vital to him as an act which influences the product he sells. Under conditions of preponderant ignorance, this asymmetry means he is much more aware of government policies that affect him as an income-earner than he is of policies that affect him as a consumer.[4]

In order to maximize its political support, the government takes account of this situation in planning its budget. It realizes that two excellent ways to gain a citizen's support are to raise his income by giving him something for nothing or to buy what he produces. But in a society with a complex division of labor, each specific income-earning group is usually a small minority of the population. Therefore government acts designed to please such a group usually distribute benefits to a minority, whereas their costs are added to the general tax burden and spread over the majority. Each recipient of such a boon thus feels he is making a net gain, since his share of the taxes added to pay for this project is much smaller than the benefit he receives. But the government also provides similar projects benefiting other minorities to which he does not belong. The costs of these projects are likewise spread over all citizens—including him—so he winds up paying for other people's special benefits, just as they pay for his. Whether or not he makes a net gain from this process is a moot point.

However, he cannot expect the government to undertake only those special projects which benefit him. Since a majority of citizens would be net losers under such an arrangement, they would vote against it. In order to get them to help pay for acts which benefit him, the government must provide them with benefits for which he helps to pay. Thus the government placates the majority who are exploited by a minority in one field by allowing them to be part of exploiting minorities in other fields.

In this process of "log-rolling," the citizens affected do not enter into direct bargains with each other. The only decision they face is which of the two competing budgets to vote for at each election. All the intervening trading of political support is done

4. The classic example of this asymmetry is the tariff. A few producers manage to get government to set protective tariffs at the expense of millions of consumers, even though politicians seek to maximize votes. This is possible because producers are much more intensely interested in their income than consumers are in the individual prices that face them. See Downs, *op.cit.*, pp. 253-257.

within the governing party, which knows that it must present the end result to the voters as a single package in competition with a similar package offered by its opponents. Each voter must then decide which budget provides him with the greatest difference between benefits received and costs imposed. If he receives many benefits from "special-interest" projects, he can expect his taxes to be swelled by the costs of similar projects benefiting other minorities, which the government must undertake to "buy off" the people who paid for his gains. Thus he might be better off if all minority benefits were eliminated and taxes lowered for everyone.

However, the question facing us is not whether budgets will include many or few minority-benefiting projects. It is whether the voters' ignorance of what is in the budget will cause governments to increase or decrease the number of such projects, thereby increasing or decreasing the budget as a whole.

As we have shown, when preponderant ignorance prevails, voters are most likely to be aware of those government policies which directly affect their sources of income. Hence they encourage government policies which raise the relative prices of the products they sell. But since any particular type of producer is in a minority in a complex society, these policies will be minority-benefiting policies. This is also true because such policies injure all buyers of the product, and buyers usually outnumber producers. Thus each citizen's perception threshold is most likely to be crossed by minority-benefiting policies involving government spending that raise (or could raise) his income.

On the other hand, government policies that affect the prices of individual goods he consumes will not be as apparent or as significant to him as policies which affect the price of what he produces. But policies that raise his costs as a consumer also benefit the citizens who produce what he consumes. It therefore appears that government can engage in specialized spending that benefits each type of producer without arousing the antagonism of consumers, especially since each consumer receives such benefits himself in his role as a producer. This situation tends to make the actual budget larger than the "correct" one.

However, this appearance is deceptive, for it ignores the cost side of the budget. When voters are preponderantly ignorant about the budget, they do not realize that special benefits are being provided to minorities to which they do not belong. But these benefits raise the general level of taxation, and voters are quite aware of their taxes, since taxes affect them directly. Thus their knowledge of the budget is narrowed down to two major items: government policies directly affecting their sources of income and those types of taxes which inherently call themselves to every citizen's attention (*e.g.*, income taxes).

As noted, when any minority gets special benefits from government spending, the minority's taxes are likely to go up much more than just its share of the cost of the benefits it receives. If the taxes that rise cannot be concealed from the citizenry, each minority may prefer to eschew its special benefits and vote for a budget which cuts out such benefits and reduces everyone's taxes. But if the taxes that rise are the type that are less likely to cross the citizens' perception threshold (*e.g.*, sales taxes), then each minority may vote for a budget which provides it with special benefits because its taxes do not appear to go up significantly.

Thus, insofar as taxation can be concealed from the electorate, the government budget will tend to be larger than the "correct" one. Voters will underestimate the costs they are paying for special benefits received, and parties will build this bias into their budgets. However, this tendency does not eliminate the previously discussed tendency toward a too-small budget. Under preponderant ignorance, both forces act simultaneously; so the net outcome in terms of total budget size is ambiguous.

THE NET RESULTS

Nevertheless, I believe the actual budget will still be smaller than the "correct" budget because even indirect taxation is much more apparent than many remote government benefits. As noted previously, whoever collects indirect taxes is aware of their existence even if in the long run he does not bear them himself. He tends to look at them as expropriation by the government of resources he could collect himself, since by raising the price of his product, they reduce his sales and cause him short-run hardships. Furthermore, he attempts to placate his customers for his higher price by identifying that element of it caused by the tax —thus making them aware of it. And if this tax is significant enough to support substantial increases over the "correct" budget, it must irritate many such persons. For these reasons, it is difficult to increase taxation to support "hidden" special projects without arousing opposition. True, policies like tariffs, which raise prices but do not increase taxes, can be used to provide minorities with hidden benefits, especially if the persons whose income-earning suffers are foreign citizens. But when a domestic appropriation of revenues is necessary to support a hidden subsidy, some voters are bound to complain. This fact necessarily limits the tendency for budgets to exceed the "correct" amount.

No such inherent brake limits the tendency for remote government benefits to be ignored. Since most remote benefits stem from preventive action, no one feels any immediate loss when they are not forthcoming. Perhaps particular producers might increase their incomes if government adopted policies that produced remote benefits, but their voices are not as loud as those of the taxpayers injured by indirect taxes. In the first place, they are not suffering "expropriation" of actual private earnings but only loss of potential income, which is rationally less significant because it must be discounted for uncertainty. Second, they are usually few compared with the large number of voters who must be taxed if the budget is to be made larger than the "correct" size. Furthermore, the benefits of preventive action in any field are usually known only to experts in that field, since such knowledge implies the ability to predict future events, which in turn demands familiarity with causal relations in the field. Whenever these experts are members of the government, they are primarily motivated to produce votes rather than benefits. But remote benefits cannot produce votes unless resources are spent to inform people about them—and voters are notoriously hard to inform about anything remote. Thus the experts who usually know most about such remote benefits are not strongly motivated to produce them—nor is anyone else.

For these reasons, the two opposite tendencies acting on the budget are not of equal strength. The forces which tend to enlarge budgets beyond the "correct" level are inherently limited, whereas those which tend to shrink it are not. Therefore I believe the budget will emerge smaller than its "correct" size. . . .

In a democracy, information costs tend to make governments enact budgets that are smaller than they would be if such costs were absent. This conclusion is true even if both parties and citizens are rational in their political behavior. It is based on the economic theory of democracy, which treats political parties as part of the division of labor, motivated primarily by self-interest like all other agents in the economy. . . .

This theory has been criticized because it cannot predict the actions of individual men, who play a central role in political events but do not always act selfishly. Therefore, it is said, the theory is useless for political analysis. But if it can reveal underlying tendencies in democracy which operate independently of individuals, then I believe it is a useful theory. In my opinion, it can be used to reach significant, nonobvious conclusions applicable to the real world—especially to the American government. I hope the analysis presented in this article provides an example of such application.

PART TWO What Role for Government Expenditure?

The Economic Functions of the State in English Classical Political Economy

Lord Robbins is Professor of Political Economy Emeritus at the London School of Economics. The Theory of Economic Policy, in which this essay appears, is a survey of the attitudes and doctrines of classical economists toward the appropriate economic functions of government.

I DO NOT think that it is any exaggeration to suggest that to-day, apart from a handful of specialists, the great body of the educated public tends to regard the Classical conception of the functions of the state as sufficiently characterized by Carlyle's phrase, "Anarchy plus the constable", or by Lassalle's simile of the night watchman. It is this view that I propose to examine.

SPECIMENS OF EXTREME INDIVIDUALISM

Now I do not question that such conceptions of the functions of the state have been widely held. At most times, in the period under discussion, it would be easy to cull from the political discussions of the day utterances and *obiter dicta* which implied just such an attitude as is suggested by Lassalle's simile. Nor am I prepared to contend that such an attitude is only to be found in the rough-and-tumble of popular controversy. On the contrary, I am clear that it is possible to discover sentiments of this sort on the lips of men who are certainly to be described as economists or social philosophers.

Take, for instance, the alleged conversation between Mercier de La Rivière and Catherine the Great. As you may know, the French economists, the Physiocrats, had a great vogue among the enlightened despots of the eighteenth century. They were invited to the various courts; their advice was solicited by the great personages. Among those who were thus distinguished was Mercier de La Rivière, the author of *L'Ordre naturel et essentiel des sociétés politiques*, which Adam Smith thought to be the best exposition of the Physiocratic system. He was asked by Catherine the Great to visit Moscow. According to Thiebault, when he arrived, the following conversation took place:

Catherine. "Sir, can you tell me the best way to govern a state?"
Mercier de La Rivière. "There is only one way, Madame. Be just, that is to say, uphold the constitution and observe the laws."
C. "But on what basis should laws be made?"
M. "On one basis only, Your Majesty, on the nature of things and of men."
C. "Most certainly. But when one wishes to make these laws what rules should be observed?"
M. "Madame, to give laws to mankind is God's prerogative. How can mere man venture on such a task? By what right would he dictate to those whom God has not placed in his hands?"
C. "To what then do you reduce the science of government?"
M. "To study the laws which God has so manifestly engraven in human society from the time of its creation. To seek to go beyond this would be a great mistake and a disastrous undertaking."
C. "Sir, it has been a great pleasure to meet you. I wish you good day." [1]

Perhaps this an over-simplified version of what actually happened; anecdotes of courts not infrequently tend that way. But no one who has read typical specimens of the Physiocratic literature would contend that it was altogether out of character.

Or take Bastiat. In his *Harmonies économiques* he lays it down that "It is the essence of government that it acts on the citizens by way of constraint. Therefore it cannot have any other rational function but the legitimate defence of individual rights, it has no authority but to make respected the liberties and the properties

1. *Souvenirs de Berlin* (2nd edition), vol. iii, pp. 167 *seq.* I owe the quotation to Oncken, *Geschichte des Nationalökonomie*, Bd. i, p. 421.

of all. . . . Beyond justice, I challenge anyone to imagine a governmental intervention which is not an injustice. . . . Thus: to preserve the public security: to administer the common domain [Rivers, Forest, Roads], to impose taxes; here, I believe, is the rational circle within which the function of government must be circumscribed or restricted. . . ." [2]

The attitude of Herbert Spencer in *Man versus the State* is of a similar order of simplicity. Of course, the object of this famous polemic is chiefly negative: the author is arguing against a trend of policy; and it is a common habit in such circumstances to tend to overstate the case. Nevertheless, it is certainly not unfair to depict him as opposed on principle to state regulation concerning health, safety and compulsory education. The regulations themselves, he argues, are usually pernicious; and the cumulative tendency is towards the servile state.

THE CLASSICAL THEORY

Thus there can be no doubt that doctrines as extreme as those pilloried by Carlyle and Lassalle have had extensive currency and the support of famous names. But they did not have the support of the Classical Economists. To identify such doctrines with the declared and easily accessible views of the Classical Economists is a sure sign of ignorance or malice. This is a strong statement, which must be supported by extensive evidence.

According to Adam Smith, the state has three functions, "first, the duty of protecting the society from the violence and invasion of other independent societies; secondly, the duty of protecting, as far as possible, every member of the society from the injustice or oppression of every other member of it; and, thirdly, [note the wording here] the duty of erecting and maintaining certain public works and certain public institutions, which it can never be for the interest of any individual, or small number of individuals, to erect and maintain; because the profit could never repay the expense to any individual or small number of individuals, though it may frequently do much more than repay it to a great society". [3]

2. Bastiat, *Œuvres complètes* (1864), vol. vi, pp. 553–555.
3. Adam Smith, *The Wealth of Nations* (Cannan's edition), vol. ii, pp. 184–185.

Before we go any further, it is interesting to compare this formulation of the functions of the state with the formulation which we find in Keynes' celebrated pamphlet *The End of Laissez-Faire*. "The most important *Agenda* of the state", says Keynes, following Bentham's terminology, "relate not to those activities which private individuals are already fulfilling, but to those functions [please note the wording again] which fall outside the sphere of the individual, to those decisions which are made by *no one* if the State does not make them. The important thing for Government is not to do things which individuals are doing already, and to do them a little better or a little worse; but to do those things which at present are not done at all." [4]

It would, of course, be misleading to suggest that the *content* of Lord Keynes' *agenda* was identical with that of Adam Smith's —control of aggregate investment and policy designed to affect the size and quality of the population were conspicuous among his illustrations—and it is quite clear that such were alien to Adam Smith's conception. But the *formal* similarity is not an accident; it indicates the essential continuity of thought in the tradition of economic liberalism concerning the positive nature of the co-operation between the state and the individual. Nor must we regard the content of Adam Smith's *agenda* as limited to provision of roads, canals, harbours and such like utilities. He made a most powerful plea for popular education and he indicated that, had he known of any available technique, he would have favoured health legislation.[5]

For the rest, we have already seen that he laid it down as a principle that those exertions of the natural liberty of a few individuals which might endanger the whole society ought to be restrained; and a careful reading of the *Wealth of Nations* will yield a very substantial number of illustrations, from quality certificates for linen and woollen cloth [6] and regulations concerning land settlement in new countries,[7] to the control of the price of bread

4. *Supra*, pp. 46–47.
5. Adam Smith, *op. cit.* vol. ii, p. 272: ". . . It would deserve its most serious attention to prevent a leprosy or any other loathsome and offensive disease, though neither mortal nor dangerous from spreading itself. . . ."
6. *Op. cit.* vol. i, p. 124.
7. *Ibid.* vol. ii, pp. 73–74.

if the supply is in the hands of a monopoly.[8] I have no desire to present a paradoxical picture of Smith as an enlightened interventionist. That would be a false perspective. But the perspective is no less false which presents him as one who would reduce the functions of the state to those of the night watchman.

I pass next to Bentham, whose significance as providing the philosophical background for the later developments has not, I think, always been fully appreciated by historians of economic thought.

If we read the famous *Be quiet* injunction to government which is also to be found in the first chapter of the *Manual of Political Economy*, we may easily be tempted to put Bentham among the extreme exponents of a negative view of state function. Although there is an explicit presumption that, over a wide field, interference is inadvisable, there is no suggestion that it is ruled out *a priori* by some system of natural rights. Bentham had no use whatever for the *Naturrecht*, and he continually goes out of his way to make this clear. Thus he is most contemptuous about those who would argue that because taxation involves a burden on those who pay it, therefore, it should be avoided. "It would . . . be a gross error, and an extremely mischievous one, to refer to the defalcation thus resulting from the mass of liberty or free agency, as affording a conclusive objection against the inter-position of the law for this or any other purpose. Every law which does not consist in the repeal, total or partial, of a coercive law, is itself a coercive law. To reprobate as a mischief resulting from this or that law, a property which is the essence of all law, is to betray . . . a total unacquaintance with what may be called the logic of the laws."[9] According to the principle of utility, as distinct from the *Naturrecht*, the expediency of any act of government must be judged solely by its consequences and not regarded as ruled out in advance by some metaphysical system of rights. In

8. *Ibid.* vol. i, p. 144.

9. Bentham, *Manual of Political Economy:* Works (ed. Bowring), vol. iii, pp. 34, 70. "In recommending freedom of trade, I suppose the minds of merchants in their sound, that is, their ordinary state. But there have been times when they acted as though they were delirious: such were the period of the Mississippi Scheme in France and the South Sea Scheme in England. The other classes of people would have had ground for seeking to divert their fellow citizens from the purchase of the smoke sold by Law, or of the *bubbles* of the South Sea."

fact, even in the *Manual* we find the most surprising examples of state action which is said to be beneficial—from accumulation, for instance, of large stocks of food against famine in circumstances where the private market does not function adequately in this respect,[10] to intervention to prevent over-speculation in stock markets.[11] He has, moreover, Adam Smith's formal argument regarding institutions involving indiscriminate benefit, illustrated *inter alia* by a justification of the building of the Caledonian Canal which might easily come from a modern work dilating on the arcana of the doctrine of external economies—though it has not the same esoteric air.[12]

But I shall give a false impression if I restrict myself to piquant examples. You get Bentham quite out of perspective if you do not think of him essentially as the great legal inventor, the greatest perhaps in history, continually seeking all along the line to erect a structure of institutions, thought out in great detail, within which action is so limited and co-ordinated as to create the good society. I wonder how many now living have ever opened the *Constitutional Code,* the great project for a practical Utopia on which Bentham lavished so much of the care and emotion of the final years of his life. Those who do, even if they restrict themselves only to the contents table, must find a picture which squares very ill with the contemporary idea of the *laissez-faire* state. Let me quote the Bentham cabinet: besides the Prime Minister:—

> Election Minister.
> Legislation Minister.
> Army Minister.
> Navy Minister.
> Preventive Service Minister (Police, Fire, etc.).
> Interior Communication Minister.
> Indigence Relief Minister.

10. *Ibid.* p. 71.
11. *Ibid.* p. 71.
12. "The justification of the communication from sea to sea through Scotland by the Caledonian Canal, is to be sought for in the same principles, though the preponderance of profit over expense can scarcely be expected to prove equally considerable. Of the profit part, though to an unassignable amount will distribute itself among a limited, and perhaps individually assignable description of individuals: other part, in portions altogether unassignable, among individuals more clearly assignable; viz. among the community at large." *Ibid.* p. 41, note.

Education Minister.
Domain Minister.
Health Minister.
Foreign Relations Minister.
Trade Minister.
Finance Minister.[13]

Pretty comprehensive is it not? When we look into the detail of the arrangements we note that care has been taken to provide a Central Statistical Office ("statistic function"), a competitively selected Civil Service, and many other administrative arrangements hardly achieved even at the present day. I confess that when I find this sort of thing I feel that, in some respects at any rate, modern practice has yet some little distance to go before it catches up with Jeremy Bentham.[14]

I must not prolong unduly this procession of witnesses. But we must not restrict ourselves to the founders: it might be argued that there had been some departure from these standards in the second and third generations. As is well known, Mill in his *Principles* devoted a whole book (Book V) to the province of government, which abounds in illustrations of what I am trying to demonstrate. It might be thought that his attitude was untypical. I prefer therefore to rely on McCulloch and Senior, of whom, on popular estimates, less of this sort of thing is to be expected.

McCulloch has a systematic discussion of the functions of government in his *Principles*. This embraces a wide field of the kind that we should expect in one who had read Smith and Bentham, and includes a strong plea for the statutory limitation of the dividends of public utility organizations. In his treatise on inheritance we may note a striking, though not untypical, repudiation of the principle of *laissez-faire*. "The principle of *laissez-faire* may be safely trusted to in some things but in many more it is wholly inapplicable; and to appeal to it on all occasions savours more of the policy of a parrot than of a statesman or a philosopher." [15]

Senior is even stronger. In his anonymous review of Mill in the *Edinburgh Review* in 1848 he poses the question, "Is it true that governments ought to confine themselves to affording protection

13. Bentham, *op. cit.* vol. ix, p. 7.
14. *Ibid.* p. 447.
15. J. R. McCulloch, *Treatise on the Succession to Property Vacant by Death* (1848), p. 156.

against force and fraud?" and comes to the conclusion that the arguments in favour of this principle "cannot be supported". He even takes exception to Mill's use of the term "optional" as applied to the function of government. "Like the words 'boon' or 'concession', it seems to imply that there may be useful measures which the government of a country may at its discretion adopt or reject." [16] And in his Oxford lectures of 1847–48 he lays it down that "the only rational foundation of government, the only foundation of a right to govern and a correlative duty to obey is, expediency—the general benefit of the community. It is the duty of a government to do whatever is conducive to the welfare of the governed. The only limit to this duty is power . . . it appears to me that the most fatal of all errors would be the general admission of the proposition that a government has no right to interfere for any purpose except for that of affording protection, for such an admission would be preventing our profiting by experience, and even from acquiring it." [17]

Unless words of this sort are to be taken as deliberate deception, they must surely be regarded as conclusive evidence against the attribution to those who used them of the night-watchman theory of the functions of government.

16. J. S. Mill's *Political Economy: Edinburgh Review*, October 1848, vol. clxxviii, p. 294 *seq*.

17. This lecture has never been published in its original form. But a snippet is given in the compilation of extracts from Senior's published and unpublished works entitled *Industrial Efficiency and Social Economy* (edited S. Leon Levy), vol. ii, p. 302.

The Role of Government in a Free Society

MILTON FRIEDMAN

Milton Friedman is Paul Russell Snowden Professor of Economics at the University of Chicago. His book, Capitalism and Freedom, *from which this essay is taken, describes competitive capitalism as a necessary condition for political freedom and defines the role that government should play in a society dedicated to freedom.*

A COMMON OBJECTION to totalitarian societies is that they regard the end as justifying the means. Taken literally, this objection is clearly illogical. If the end does not justify the means, what does? But this easy answer does not dispose of the objection; it simply shows that the objection is not well put. To deny that the end justifies the means is indirectly to assert that the end in question is not the ultimate end, that the ultimate end is itself the use of the proper means. Desirable or not, any end that can be attained only by the use of bad means must give way to the more basic end of the use of acceptable means.

To the liberal, the appropriate means are free discussion and voluntary cooperation, which implies that any form of coercion is inappropriate. The ideal is unanimity among responsible individuals achieved on the basis of free and full discussion.

From this standpoint, the role of the market is that it permits unanimity without conformity; that it is a system of effectively proportional representation. On the other hand, the characteristic feature of action through explicitly political channels is that it tends to require or to enforce substantial conformity. The typical issue must be decided "yes" or "no"; at most, provision can be made for a fairly limited number of alternatives. Even the use of proportional representation in its explicitly political form does not alter this conclusion. The number of separate groups that can in fact be represented is narrowly limited, enormously so by comparison with the proportional representation of the market. More important, the fact that the final outcome generally must be a law applicable to all groups, rather than separate legisla-

tive enactments for each "party" represented, means that proportional representation in its political version, far from permit-
ting unanimity without conformity, tends toward ineffectiveness
and fragmentation. It thereby operates to destroy any consensus
on which unanimity with conformity can rest.

There are clearly some matters with respect to which effective
proportional representation is impossible. I cannot get the
amount of national defense I want and you, a different amount.
With respect to such indivisible matters we can discuss, and
argue, and vote. But having decided, we must conform. It is
precisely the existence of such indivisible matters—protection
of the individual and the nation from coercion are clearly the
most basic—that prevents exclusive reliance on individual action
through the market. If we are to use some of our resources for
such indivisible items, we must employ political channels to
reconcile differences.

The use of political channels, while inevitable, tends to strain
the social cohesion essential for a stable society. The strain is
least if agreement for joint action need be reached only on a
limited range of issues on which people in any event have common views. Every extension of the range of issues for which
explicit agreement is sought strains further the delicate threads
that hold society together. If it goes so far as to touch an issue
on which men feel deeply yet differently, it may well disrupt
the society. Fundamental differences in basic values can seldom
if ever be resolved at the ballot box; ultimately they can only
be decided, though not resolved, by conflict. The religious and
civil wars of history are a bloody testament to this judgment.

The widespread use of the market reduces the strain on the
social fabric by rendering conformity unnecessary with respect
to any activities it encompasses. The wider the range of activities
covered by the market, the fewer are the issues on which explicitly political decisions are required and hence on which it is
necessary to achieve agreement. In turn, the fewer the issues on
which agreement is necessary, the greater is the likelihood of
getting agreement while maintaining a free society.

Unanimity is, of course, an ideal. In practice, we can afford
neither the time nor the effort that would be required to achieve
complete unanimity on every issue. We must perforce accept
something less. We are thus led to accept majority rule in one

form or another as an expedient. That majority rule is an expedient rather than itself a basic principle is clearly shown by the fact that our willingness to resort to majority rule, and the size of the majority we require, themselves depend on the seriousness of the issue involved. If the matter is of little moment and the minority has no strong feelings about being overruled, a bare plurality will suffice. On the other hand, if the minority feels strongly about the issue involved, even a bare majority will not do. Few of us would be willing to have issues of free speech, for example, decided by a bare majority. Our legal structure is full of such distinctions among kinds of issues that require different kinds of majorities. At the extreme are those issues embodied in the Constitution. These are the principles that are so important that we are willing to make minimal concessions to expediency. Something like essential consensus was achieved initially in accepting them, and we require something like essential consensus for a change in them.

The self-denying ordinance to refrain from majority rule on certain kinds of issues that is embodied in our Constitution and in similar written or unwritten constitutions elsewhere, and the specific provisions in these constitutions or their equivalents prohibiting coercion of individuals, are themselves to be regarded as reached by free discussion and as reflecting essential unanimity about means.

I turn now to consider more specifically, though still in very broad terms, what the areas are that cannot be handled through the market at all, or can be handled only at so great a cost that the use of political channels may be preferable.

GOVERNMENT AS RULE-MAKER AND UMPIRE

It is important to distinguish the day-to-day activities of people from the general customary and legal framework within which these take place. The day-to-day activities are like the actions of the participants in a game when they are playing it; the framework, like the rules of the game they play. And just as a good game requires acceptance by the players both of the rules and of the umpire to interpret and enforce them, so a good society requires that its members agree on the general conditions that will govern relations among them, on some means of arbitrating different interpretations of these conditions, and on some device for enforcing compliance with the generally accepted rules. As in games, so also in society, most of the general conditions are the unintended outcome of custom, accepted unthinkingly. At most, we consider explicitly only minor modifications in them, though the cumulative effect of a series of minor modifications may be a drastic alteration in the character of the game or of the society. In both games and society also, no set of rules can prevail unless most participants most of the time conform to them without external sanctions; unless that is, there is a broad underlying social consensus. But we cannot rely on custom or on this consensus alone to interpret and to enforce the rules; we need an umpire. These then are the basic roles of government in a free society: to provide a means whereby we can modify the rules, to mediate differences among us on the meaning of the rules, and to enforce compliance with the rules on the part of those few who would otherwise not play the game.

The need for government in these respects arises because absolute freedom is impossible. However attractive anarchy may be as a philosophy, it is not feasible in a world of imperfect men. Men's freedoms can conflict, and when they do, one man's freedom must be limited to preserve another's—as a Supreme Court Justice once put it, "My freedom to move my fist must be limited by the proximity of your chin."

The major problem in deciding the appropriate activities of government is how to resolve such conflicts among the freedoms of different individuals. In some cases, the answer is easy. There is little difficulty in attaining near unanimity to the proposition that one man's freedom to murder his neighbor must be sacrificed to preserve the freedom of the other man to live. In other cases, the answer is difficult. In the economic area, a major problem arises in respect of the conflict between freedom to combine and freedom to compete. What meaning is to be attributed to "free" as modifying "enterprise"? In the United States, "free" has been understood to mean that anyone is free to set up an enterprise, which means that existing enterprises are not free to keep out competitors except by selling a better product at the same price or the same product at a lower price. In the continental tradition, on the other hand, the meaning has generally been that enterprises are free to do what they want, including the fixing of prices, division of markets, and the adoption of other techniques to keep out potential competitors. Perhaps the most difficult specific problem in this area arises with respect to combinations among laborers, where the problem of freedom to combine and freedom to compete is particularly acute.

A still more basic economic area in which the answer is both difficult and important is the definition of property rights. The notion of property, as it has developed over centuries and as it is embodied in our legal codes, has become so much a part of us that we tend to take it for granted, and fail to recognize the extent to which just what constitutes property and what rights the ownership of property confers are complex social creations rather than self-evident propositions. Does my having title to land, for example, and my freedom to use my property as I wish, permit me to deny to someone else the right to fly over my land in his airplane? Or does his right to use his airplane take precedence? Or does this depend on how high he flies? Or how much noise he makes? Does voluntary exchange require that he pay me for the privilege of flying over my land? Or that I must pay him to refrain from flying over it? The mere mention of royalties, copyrights, patents; shares of stock in corporations; riparian rights, and the like, may perhaps emphasize the role of generally accepted social rules in the very definition of property. It may suggest also that, in many cases, the existence of a well specified and generally accepted definition of property is far more important than just what the definition is. . . .

In summary, the organization of economic activity through voluntary exchange presumes that we have provided, through government, for the maintenance of law and order to prevent coercion of one individual by another, the enforcement of contracts voluntarily entered into, the definition of the meaning of property rights, the interpretation and enforcement of such rights, and the provision of a monetary framework.

ACTION THROUGH GOVERNMENT ON GROUNDS OF
TECHNICAL MONOPOLY AND NEIGHBORHOOD EFFECTS

The role of government just considered is to do something that the market cannot do for itself, namely, to determine, arbitrate, and enforce the rules of the game. We may also want to do through government some things that might conceivably be done through the market but that technical or similar conditions render it difficult to do in that way. These all reduce to cases in which strictly voluntary exchange is either exceedingly costly or practically impossible. There are two general classes of such cases: monopoly and similar market imperfections, and neighborhood effects.

Exchange is truly voluntary only when nearly equivalent alternatives exist. Monopoly implies the absence of alternatives and thereby inhibits effective freedom of exchange. In practice, monopoly frequently, if not generally, arises from government support or from collusive agreements among individuals. With respect to these, the problem is either to avoid governmental fostering of monopoly or to stimulate the effective enforcement of rules such as those embodied in our antitrust laws. However, monopoly may also arise because it is technically efficient to have a single producer or enterprise. I venture to suggest that such cases are more limited than is supposed but they unquestionably do arise. A simple example is perhaps the provision of telephone services within a community. I shall refer to such cases as "technical" monopoly.

When technical conditions make a monopoly the natural outcome of competitive market forces, there are only three alternatives that seem available: private monopoly, public monopoly, or public regulation. All three are bad so we must choose among evils. Henry Simons, observing public regulation of monopoly in the United States, found the results so distasteful that he concluded public monopoly would be a lesser evil. Walter Eucken, a noted German liberal, observing public monopoly in German railroads, found the results so distasteful that he concluded public regulation would be a lesser evil. Having learned from both, I reluctantly conclude that, if tolerable, private monopoly may be the least of the evils.

If society were static so that the conditions which give rise to a technical monopoly were sure to remain, I would have little confidence in this solution. In a rapidly changing society, however, the conditions making for technical monopoly frequently change and I suspect that both public regulation and public monopoly are likely to be less responsive to such changes in conditions, to be less readily capable of elimination, than private monopoly.

Railroads in the United States are an excellent example. A large degree of monopoly in railroads was perhaps inevitable on technical grounds in the nineteenth century. This was the justification for the Interstate Commerce Commission. But conditions have changed. The emergence of road and air transport has reduced the monopoly element in railroads to negligible proportions. Yet we have not eliminated the ICC. On the contrary, the ICC, which started out as an agency to protect the public from exploitation by the railroads, has become an agency to protect railroads from competition by trucks and other means of transport, and more recently even to protect existing truck companies from competition by new entrants. Similarly, in England, when the railroads were nationalized, trucking was at first brought into the state monopoly. If railroads had never been subjected to regulation in the United States, it is nearly certain that by now transportation, including railroads, would be a highly competitive industry with little or no remaining monopoly elements.

The choice among the evils of private monopoly, public monopoly, and public regulation cannot, however, be made once and for all, independently of the factual circumstances. If the technical monopoly is of a service or commodity that is regarded as essential and if its monopoly power is sizable, even the short-run effects of private unregulated monopoly may not be tolerable, and either public regulation or ownership may be a lesser evil.

Technical monopoly may on occasion justify a *de facto* public monopoly. It cannot by itself justify a public monopoly achieved by making it illegal for anyone else to compete. For example, there is no way to justify our present public monopoly of the post office. It may be argued that the carrying of mail is a technical monopoly and that a government monopoly is the least of evils. Along these lines, one could perhaps justify a government post office but not the present law, which makes it illegal for anybody else to carry mail. If the delivery of mail is a technical monopoly, no one will be able to succeed in competition with the government. If it is not, there is no reason why the government should be engaged in it. The only way to find out is to leave other people free to enter.

The historical reason why we have a post office monopoly is because the Pony Express did such a good job of carrying the mail across the continent that, when the government introduced transcontinental service, it couldn't compete effectively and lost money. The result was a law making it illegal for anybody else to carry the mail. That is why the Adams Express Company is an investment trust today instead of an operating company. I conjecture that if entry into the mail-carrying business were open to all, there would be a large number of firms entering it and this archaic industry would become revolutionized in short order.

A second general class of cases in which strictly voluntary exchange is impossible arises when actions of individuals have effects on other individuals for which it is not feasible to charge or recompense them. This is the problem of "neighborhood effects." An obvious example is the pollution of a stream. The man who pollutes a stream is in effect forcing others to exchange good water for bad. These others might be willing to make the exchange at a price. But it is not feasible for them, acting individually, to avoid the exchange or to enforce appropriate compensation.

A less obvious example is the provision of highways. In this case, it is technically possible to identify and hence charge individuals for their use of the roads and so to have private operation. However, for general access roads, involving many points of entry and exit, the costs of collection would be extremely high if a charge were to be made for the specific services received by each individual, because of the necessity of establishing toll booths or the equivalent at all entrances. The gasoline tax is a much cheaper method of charging individuals roughly in proportion to their use of the roads. This method, however, is one in which the particular payment cannot be identified closely with the particular use. Hence, it is hardly feasible to have private enterprise provide the service and collect the charge without establishing extensive private monopoly.

These considerations do not apply to long-distance turnpikes with high density of traffic and limited access. For these, the costs of collection are small and in many cases are now being paid, and there are often numerous alternatives, so that there is no serious monopoly problem. Hence, there is every reason why these should be privately owned and operated. If so owned and operated, the enterprise running the highway should receive the gasoline taxes paid on account of travel on it.

Parks are an interesting example because they illustrate the difference between cases that can and cases that cannot be justified by neighborhood effects, and because almost everyone at first sight regards the conduct of national parks as obviously a valid function of government. In fact, however, neighborhood effects may justify a city park; they do not justify a national park, like Yellowstone National Park or the Grand Canyon. What is the fundamental difference between the two? For the city park, it is extremely difficult to identify the people who benefit from it and to charge them for the benefits which they receive. If there is a park in the middle of the city, the houses on all sides get the benefit of the open space, and people who walk through it or by it also benefit. To maintain toll collectors at the gates or to impose annual charges per window overlooking the park would be very expensive and difficult. The entrances to a national park like Yellowstone, on the other hand, are few; most of the people who came stay for a considerable period of time and it is perfectly feasible to set up toll gates and collect admission charges. This is indeed now done, though the charges do not cover the whole costs. If the public wants this kind of an activity enough to pay for it, private enterprises will have every incentive to provide such parks. And, of course, there are many private enterprises of this nature now in existence. I cannot myself conjure up any neighborhood effects or important monopoly effects that would justify governmental activity in this area.

Considerations like those I have treated under the heading of neighborhood effects have been used to rationalize almost every conceivable intervention. In many instances, however, this rationalization is special pleading rather than a legitimate application of the concept of neighborhood effects. Neighborhood effects cut both ways. They can be a reason for limiting the activities of government as well as for expanding them. Neighborhood effects impede voluntary exchange because it is difficult to identify the effects on third parties and to measure their magnitude; but this difficulty is present in governmental activity as well. It is hard to know when neighborhood effects are sufficiently large to justify particular costs in overcoming them and even harder to distribute the costs in an appropriate fashion. Consequently, when government engages in activities to overcome neighborhood effects, it will in part introduce an additional set of neighborhood effects by failing to charge or to compensate individuals properly. Whether the original or the new neighborhood effects are the more serious can only be judged by the facts of the individual case, and even then, only very approximately. Furthermore, the use of government to overcome neighborhood effects itself has an extremely important neighborhood effect which is unrelated to the particular occasion for government action. Every act of government intervention limits the area of individual freedom directly and threatens the preservation of freedom indirectly.

Our principles offer no hard and fast line how far it is appropriate to use government to accomplish jointly what it is difficult or impossible for us to accomplish separately through strictly voluntary exchange. In any particular case of proposed intervention, we must make up a balance sheet, listing separately the advantages and disadvantages. Our principles tell us what items to put on the one side and what items on the other and they give us some basis for attaching importance to the different items. In particular, we shall always want to enter on the liability side of any proposed government intervention its neighborhood effect in threatening freedom and give this effect considerable weight. Just how much weight to give to it, as to other items, depends upon the circumstances. If, for example, existing government intervention is minor, we shall attach a smaller weight to the negative effects of additional government intervention. This is an important reason why many earlier liberals, like Henry Simons, writing at a time when government was small by today's standards, were willing to have government undertake activities that today's liberals would not accept now that government has become so overgrown.

ACTION THROUGH GOVERNMENT ON PATERNALISTIC GROUNDS

Freedom is a tenable objective only for responsible individuals. We do not believe in freedom for madmen or children. The necessity of drawing a line between responsible individuals and others is inescapable, yet it means that there is an essential ambiguity in our ultimate objective of freedom. Paternalism is inescapable for those whom we designate as not responsible.

The clearest case, perhaps, is that of madmen. We are willing neither to permit them freedom nor to shoot them. It would be nice if we could rely on voluntary activities of individuals to house and care for the madmen. But I think we cannot rule out the possibility that such charitable activities will be inadequate, if only because of the neighborhood effect involved in the fact that I benefit if another man contributes to the care of the insane. For this reason, we may be willing to arrange for their care through government.

Children offer a more difficult case. The ultimate operative unit in our society is the family, not the individual. Yet the acceptance of the family as the unit rests in considerable part on expediency rather than principle. We believe that parents are generally best able to protect their children and to provide for their development into responsible individuals for whom freedom is appropriate. But we do not believe in the freedom of parents to do what they will with other people. The children are responsible individuals in embryo, and a believer in freedom believes in protecting their ultimate rights.

To put this in a different and what may seem a more callous way, children are at one and the same time consumer goods and potentially responsible members of society. The freedom of individuals to use their economic resources as they want includes the freedom to use them to have children—to buy, as it were, the services of children as a particular form of consumption. But once this choice is exercised, the children have a value in and of themselves and have a freedom of their own that is not simply an extension of the freedom of the parents.

The paternalistic ground for governmental activity is in many ways the most troublesome to a liberal; for it involves the acceptance of a principle—that some shall decide for others—which he finds objectionable in most applications and which he rightly regards as a hallmark of his chief intellectual opponents, the proponents of collectivism in one or another of its guises, whether it be communism, socialism, or a welfare state. Yet there is no use pretending that problems are simpler than in fact they are. There is no avoiding the need for some measure of paternalism. As Dicey wrote in 1914 about an act for the protection of mental defectives, "The Mental Deficiency Act is the first step along a path on which no sane man can decline to enter, but which, if too far pursued, will bring statesmen across difficulties hard to meet without considerable interference with individual liberty." [1] There is no formula that can tell us where to stop. We must rely on our fallible judgment and, having reached a judgment, on our ability to persuade our fellow men that it is a correct judgment, or their ability to persuade us to modify our views. We must put our faith, here as elsewhere, in a consensus reached by imperfect and biased men through free discussion and trial and error.

CONCLUSION

A government which maintained law and order, defined property rights, served as a means whereby we could modify property rights and other rules of the economic game, adjudicated disputes about the interpretation of the rules, enforced contracts, promoted competition, provided a monetary framework, engaged in activities to counter technical monopolies and to overcome neighborhood effects widely regarded as sufficiently important to justify government intervention, and which supplemented private charity and the private family in protecting the irresponsible, whether madman or child—such a government would clearly have important functions to perform. The consistent liberal is not an anarchist.

Yet it is also true that such a government would have clearly limited functions and would refrain from a host of activities that are now undertaken by federal and state governments in the United States, and their counterparts in other Western countries. It may help to give a sense of proportion about the role that a liberal would assign government simply to list some activities currently undertaken by government in the U.S. that cannot, so far as I can see, validly be justified in terms of the principles outlined above:

1. Parity-price-support programs for agriculture.
2. Tariffs on imports or restrictions on exports, such as current

1. A. V. Dicey, *Lectures on the Relation between Law and Public Opinion in England during the Nineteenth Century*, 2d. ed. (London: Macmillan & Co., 1914), p. li.

oil import quotas, sugar quotas, etc.

3. Governmental control of output, such as through the farm program or through prorationing of oil as is done by the Texas Railroad Commission.

4. Rent control, such as is still practiced in New York, and more general price and wage controls such as were imposed during and just after World War II.

5. Legal minimum wage rates, or legal maximum prices, such as the legal maximum of zero on the rate of interest that can be paid on demand deposits by commercial banks, or the legally fixed maximum rates that can be paid on savings and time deposits.

6. Detailed regulation of industries, such as the regulation of transportation by the Interstate Commerce Commission. This had some justification on technical monopoly grounds when initially introduced for railroads; it has none now for any means of transport. Another example is detailed regulation of banking.

7. A similar example, but one which deserves special mention because of its implicit censorship and violation of free speech, is the control of radio and television by the Federal Communications Commission.

8. Present social security programs, especially the old-age and retirement programs compelling people in effect (a) to spend a specified fraction of their income on the purchase of retirement annuity and (b) to buy the annuity from a publicly operated enterprise.

9. Licensure provisions in various cities and states which restrict particular enterprises or occupations or professions to people who have a license, where the license is more than a receipt for a tax which anyone who wishes to enter the activity may pay.

10. So-called "public-housing" and the host of other subsidy programs directed at fostering residential construction such as FHA and V.A. guarantee of mortgage, and the like.

11. Conscription to man the military services in peacetime. The appropriate free-market arrangement is volunteer military forces; which is to say, hiring men to serve. There is no justification for not paying whatever prices is necessary to attract the required number of men. Present arrangements

are inequitable and arbitrary, seriously interfere with the freedom of young men to shape their lives, and probably are even more costly than the market alternative. (Universal military training to provide a reserve for wartime is a different problem and may be justified on liberal grounds.)

12. National parks, as noted above.
13. The legal prohibition on the carrying of mail for profit.
14. Publicly owned and operated toll roads, as noted above.

This list is far from comprehensive.

Government and the Sovereign Consumer

FRANCIS M. BATOR

Francis M. Bator is Associate Professor of Economics at the Massachusetts Institute of Technology. His book The Question of Government Spending *constructs a case for public expenditure on the ground that private enterprise cannot satisfactorily meet the whole range of consumer wants.*

Is, OR is not, the consumer to be sovereign? If we believe that the objective of economic activity is to cater to the individual consumer, then, it is argued, we must abide by the allocations implied by consumers' tastes as revealed by their market choices. Absorption of resources by paternalistic activities which do not meet a market "test" is prima facie illegitimate; and, while it must be tolerated as the lesser of evils as regards provision for defense, the administration of jails, and other "obviously" public activities, any shift of resources from private to public use is to be deplored irrespective of how much you and I may prefer more public hospitals to more automobiles. Or so the argument goes.

In fact, few people believe in the doctrine of consumer sovereignty in its pure, unadulterated form. But what if everyone did? What if we could all agree that consumers' preferences are the only admissible touchstone for economic performance—that we will suppress any qualms about attributing ultimate significance to people's television-bombarded tastes for appliances (and disregard all difficulties with children and the insane and all problems of technical ignorance)? Would it follow that there is no need for allocating resources through political decision? Or does the very doctrine of consumer sovereignty impose on government, aside from its income distribution, stabilization, and general policing functions, an obligation partially to short-circuit market processes in the allocation of resources?[1]

---

1. Even if the answer were in the negative—if there were no narrowly "economic" case for allocation by government—one could not rule out preference for modes of organization other than laissez-faire markets on quite different grounds. A fastidious humanitarian, for instance, might

A DIGRESSION ON MARKET EFFICIENCY

The negative contention—that there is no call for allocation by government—stands or falls with the crucial premise of the laissez-faire position, notably that a price-market system is such an efficient instrument for inducing consumers to reveal their preferences and producers to cater to these that allocations not subjected to a market test are bound to do worse by consumers than allocations which pass such a test. Is this so with regard to all activities? What is there of truth and error in the notion of market efficiency? [2]

The full answer, as it has emerged during the course of a century and a half of polemics and careful analysis, is unavoidably technical, being based on perhaps the most subtle insights of modern economic theory.[3] Yet its essence is simple enough. Imagine a world (1) where each individual's market choices reflect a subjective *preference ordering* which permits him to register

---

argue that to organize society so as to take advantage of man's instinct for material self-aggrandizement is bound to demean the human spirit and hence is immoral, no matter how much more efficient such organization may be in catering to "standard of living" values. On the other hand, a European-type liberal may hold that a variety of political and social non-output values relating to the configuration of power, opportunity, etc., are so much better served by some form of even grossly inefficient market institutions than by possible alternative modes of more efficient organization as to warrant choice of the former. But these are different matters; here my concern is with a price-market system not as an end, nor even as a means to noneconomic political and ethical ends, but simply as an organizational device for catering to consumers' wants. In particular, I am not concerned with the right "freely" to choose in markets.

2. In the notion, to take a significant recent formulation, that "when it comes to the advancing and expanding of our economy, that is by and large the business of Americans; the federal government can help, but . . . *our federal money will never be spent so intelligently and in so useful a fashion for the economy as will the expenditures that would be made by the private citizen, the taxpayer, if he hadn't had so much of it funneled off into the Federal Government.*" (President Eisenhower, January 14, 1959, cited in Transcript of News Conference, *New York Times*, January 15, 1959, p. 18; my italics.)

3. And on a line of thought that goes back to Adam Smith, Ricardo, Mill, Walras, and Marshall. Important modern contributions have been made by Vilfredo Pareto, Enrico Barone, Knut Wicksell, and Professor A. C. Pigou, all writing just before World War I, and more recently by Abram Bergson, A. P. Lerner, and Paul Samuelson, and by H. Hotelling, J. R. Hicks, and Oscar Lange. For a detailed technical exposition, see my "The Simple Analytics of Welfare Maximization," *American Economic Review*, March 1957, pp 22–59. [For a simpler exposition see, for example, P. A. Samuelson, *Economics*, 5th edition (New York: McGraw-Hill, 1961),

preference or indifference as between any two bundles of goods and services independently of any other person's choices; (2) where the input-output decisions of each producer—his decisions about how much labor and raw material to buy, what machines to use, how much of what to produce, etc.—reflect a single-minded urge to maximize profit, subject only to the state of the production arts and market prices; and (3) where there exist very many independent buyers and sellers in every market, and hence a state of perfect competition. It can be shown that in such a world the particular allocation and distribution of scarce resources brought about by the separate decisions of millions of profit-maximizing producers and by the consumption and leisure-work decisions of millions of consumers, all facing competitively determined prices in every market, will tend to be *efficient*. In what sense? In the very special sense that there will remain no possible reallocations, no shifts in inputs, outputs, and in distribution *such as would make some one or more individuals better off in terms of their own preferences without making some other individuals worse off in terms of theirs*. . . .

[Given these assumptions] about the independence of preferences and the feasibility of perfect competition, markets will yield efficient solutions. Each producer, concerned only with his own profit, and each consumer, bent on getting the most out of what he has, will do precisely what is needed to exhaust all mutually advantageous reallocations. Just this, in fact, is the sum and substance of Adam Smith's famed theorem of the "invisible hand." [4]

It would not be appropriate here—sadly, because it is a thing of beauty—to set out in detail the analytical content of the theorem. Its kernel lies in the remarkable fact that the mathematics of solving the problem of efficiency makes use of a set of auxiliary variables ("unknowns") *which turn out to have all the earmarks of prices, wage rates, interest rates, and rents*. This in the double sense that (1) the computational procedure involved in finding an efficient combination of inputs, outputs, and distribution hap-

pp.608–9, 678–89; also, Oscar Lange and F. M. Taylor, *On the Economic Theory of Socialism* (Minneapolis: University of Minnesota, 1938), pp. 57–90. *Editor*.]

4. In precise technical language, the theorem asserts that the equilibrium conditions which characterize a system of perfectly competitive markets will, given our assumptions, exactly correspond to the conditions implied by the solution of the mathematical maximizing problem which defines efficiency.

pens to yield, as a by-product, numerical magnitudes for these auxiliary variables which correspond precisely to the prices on which competitive markets would settle to cause supply to match demand in every market; and (2) that profit- and preference-maximizing decisions by millions of producers and consumers, all responding to these price numbers, would yield just that pattern of inputs, outputs, and distribution which the mathematical solution of the efficiency problem calls for. What this implies is that the rules followed, e.g., by competing producers bent on maximizing their own profits, are precisely the rules they must follow if allocation is to be efficient. *Example:* a profit-eager producer facing competitively determined prices will increase his output up to where the increase in total cost due to the last unit. i.e., *marginal cost,* just equals the increase in revenue he can get by selling the last unit, i.e., price. But marginal-cost-equal-to-price can be shown to be just the rule producers *must* follow if their input-output decisions are to lead to efficient allocation.

WHAT ROLE FOR GOVERNMENT SPENDING?

If a price-market "game" is a flawlessly efficient computing device with a more or less workable institutional counterpart, what sense is there in bypassing markets? [The question we ask is whether there is] a case for government spending even in a world of single-minded and error-free profit- and preference-maximizing calculations, where consumers' tastes are really all that count.

Transfer Payments [5] · How are dollar votes to be distributed among people? The ethical postulate that we should do as well as possible by consumers' tastes provides no answer. It is neutral as among the *infinite* number of efficient solutions, which range from all food and all clothing going to Crusoe to where everything goes to Friday.

Choice among efficient combinations involves ultimate ethical values (call them "equity values"), and it would be sheer accident if the particular efficient configuration generated by markets turned out to rate higher in terms of my ethical valuations, or yours, or Thomas Jefferson's, or that of a politically engineered

5. Recall that transfer payments redistribute income but do not constitute a claim on resources.

"consensus," than all other efficient, and even many inefficient, solutions. It is evidently not true that to secure the efficiency vouchsafed by competitive markets we must accept the distribution of income generated by such markets. It is possible to break the link between ownership and "final" income distribution by means of tax-financed interpersonal "transfers" and to do so without exempting any allocations from a private market test. In fact, this is precisely what is done. Government spending on old-age assistance, on veterans' cash bonuses, and the like does not cause resources to bypass markets; it simply redistributes command over resources among people. The final spending for goods and services is by private individuals bidding in markets, guided by their personal preferences.[6]

Exhaustive Expenditure and Subsidies · The case for or against pure transfer expenditure cannot be resolved, it appears, by invoking the doctrine of consumer sovereignty; explicit attention must be given to the ethics and politics of income distribution. But what about government purchases of goods and services and subsidies? Is there any justification, in terms of the principle of efficiently catering to consumers' tastes, for bypassing a market test and allocating some resources via political procedures?[7]

The answer hangs on the validity of the assumptions about preferences and conditions of production which are necessary for the "invisible hand" theorem to hold. In the above discussion of market efficiency, these assumptions, while repeatedly mentioned, were treated rather lightly. Yet it is the failure of the assumptions even approximately to match the facts of the real world that constitutes the core of the strictly "economic" case for

6. It is a different matter that some hold any such redistribution wrong on *ethical* grounds, as violating the "natural right" of everyone to his property, or to what he earns, or to what he is "worth" on the market. To ascribe ethical significance to the particular distribution of income effected by markets is to introduce a value judgment over and above the value of efficiently catering to consumers' tastes.

7. Or, in the case of subsidies, of modifying the effect of the market test? [In a later paragraph, Bator states, "With direct interaction of preferences, decentralization of allocation decisions via flawlessly competitive markets can no longer be assumed costless; private decisions will waste opportunities for making some people better off without hurting others." This condition, which Bator assumes away for the sake of argument, would justify government subsidies and possibly expenditures. *Editor.*]

public spending.[8] If we care about consumers' preferences, we must cope with two related technical characteristics of the real world which cause decentralized market calculation to be grossly inefficient—economies of scale in production, and the prevalence of what the economist calls "public goods."

Where the "Invisible Hand" Fails (1) · Competition requires that there be "very many" producers in every market. If economies of large-scale production confer a cost advantage on firms that are large relative to the total market, a few technically efficient producers will saturate the market, and competition, in the technical sense, will break down. Each producer will be large enough for his *own* output decisions to have an appreciable effect on price. This in turn will cause the profit-minded producer to fix his output at a level where marginal cost is less than price, i.e., at a level lower than is required for efficient allocation. Output will fall short of where the extra cost to society is just covered by extra benefit as measured by price.[9]

Nor can antitrust action, no matter how ideally designed, cor-

---

8. That such an "economic" case is too narrow a foundation for even an "economic" theory of government is almost too obvious to warrant comment. Indeed, some may feel that to explore what justification there may be for government spending in terms of the ethical postulates of Manchester liberalism is a foolish waste of time, especially since it requires that we take a rather abstract view of markets. Yet quite apart from the analytical insight the exercise may offer, it is not clear to me that the "Manchester view" either is, or indeed that it ought to be, so dead as to warrant the charge of irrelevance.

9. The technical reason is simple enough. While, for *efficient* allocation, output should be increased up to where the extra cost of the last unit just equals the *price* people are willing to pay, the producer is interested in the balance between extra cost and extra (i.e., *marginal*) revenue. In a competitive market where, to take an example, an increase in a single farmer's output will not appreciably reduce the price of wheat, the extra revenue that accrues to the farmer if he sells an extra bushel is just equal to the price. But where a single producer is large enough relative to the market to take account of the effect on price of changes in his *own* output, his marginal revenue will no longer equal price. Marginal revenue on, say, the 101st unit of output will equal, rather, the price on the 101st *less* the reduction in revenue (i.e., the sales value) on the first 100 units due to the drop in market price which is caused by throwing the 101st unit on the market. Hence at the level of output at which the producer's total profit is at a maximum, i.e., where the extra revenue due to the last unit is just equal to the extra cost, such extra (marginal) cost will be less than price. People would be willing to pay more for an additional unit of output than the extra cost involved in producing it.

rect the situation. While useful in controlling or eliminating concentration of market power which is based on other than technical or administrative economies of large-scale production (e.g., concentration based on financial advantages of size due to imperfections in capital markets), trying to maintain many small units if there are true resource economies to be had by large-scale production is obviously a self-defeating procedure.[10]

Price regulation of the right sort, as approximated by the best public utility commissions, is more akin to what is needed. A publicly administered price, if it allows for positive profit, will induce as-if competitive behavior. For maximum profit, output will be increased up to where marginal cost is just covered by the centrally fixed price. But even this fails to get at the heart of the matter. It fails, notably, to take account of the curious fact that the price-output combination required for efficient allocation may well imply negative profits, i.e., continuing losses.

The key to this paradox lies in the meaning of "economies of scale." The existence of scale economies at a given level of output means no more nor less than that a small increase in output from that level will cause unit cost (cost per unit: total cost divided by output) to fall. It happens, moreover, that at such a point of declining *unit* cost, marginal cost: the increment in total cost due to an extra unit of output, is necessarily less than unit cost.[11] Yet it is generally still true that, if allocation is to be efficient, output must be increased up to where marginal cost is just covered by price. But if price is to equal marginal cost where marginal cost is less than unit cost, price must be less than unit cost. Evidently efficiency requires that producers operating in a

10. This is not to gainsay that antitrust measures can reduce some of the undesirable effects of concentration. But their proper role is not to try to maintain the world as it would be if perfect competition were feasible. Rather, it is to serve as one of a variety of complementary instruments of social control appropriate to a world where perfect competition is not feasible.

11. In fact, it is the difference between *marginal* cost and *unit* cost that causes unit cost to fall as output is increased. If unit cost were $1.00 and marginal cost $1.00, why should unit cost fall? The increase in total cost due to an extra unit of output would be $1.00 and unit cost, i.e., total cost divided by output, would remain $1.00. But if unit cost at an output of 20 units is $1.00, while the increase in total cost due to the 21st unit is only $.50, the unit cost of 21 units would be $\frac{20 \times \$1 + 1 \times \$.50}{21} =$ $\frac{\$20.50}{21}$, or less than $1.00.

range of decreasing cost operate at a loss. Evidently, also, no profit-seeking producer will long do so.[12]

Consider, for example, the "production" of bridge crossings. Assume, to take an extreme instance, that once the bridge in question is built, all wear and tear is a function of time rather than use, i.e., that there are no additional costs associated with extra crossings. (The bridge is never so full as to give rise to crowding.) The marginal cost to society, in terms of scarce resources, of an additional crossing is zero. It follows—the proposition is mathematically demonstrable, as well as, in this case, intuitively obvious—that the efficient ration price for a crossing is precisely zero. A positive price such as would discourage even a single crossing would cause allocation to be inefficient; there would remain unexploited a costless crossing which could make someone better off without hurting anyone else. Yet it is equally evident that charging a price of zero for crossings will hardly raise sufficient revenue to cover the cost of building the bridge.

It is tempting to argue that if this is the case, if the bridge cannot pay for itself, then it should not be built. But this is not even plausible. It implies that no facility with a large fixed (initial) cost and relatively low *variable* cost (and therefore low marginal cost) should ever be built. (It is just such high fixed-cost and low variable-cost facilities that are characterized by unit costs which decline with output; it is simply a matter of spreading the "fixed" overhead.) Not only bridges but also roads, railroads, airfields, dams, ports, would all be ruled out as uneconomic. But of course the proposition is indefensible. It is easy to prove that where technology gives rise to economies of scale at the relevant levels of output, profitability at a competitive price is not a necessary condition of efficiency. The test of profit breaks down.[13]

12. Where market imperfections are pervasive, there are also other difficulties with the rule that output be increased to where marginal cost equals price. If one is trying to get nine drunks who are tied to each other to walk in a straight line, it may not help to sober up one of them.

13. To a sophisticated businessman used to running a decentralized multi-division firm all this would not come as too much of a surprise. Not every process in a well-run firm should be expected to cover its cost in terms of the right set of internal accounting prices. *Total* profit is the deciding criterion, and it may be worth while for a firm to build a private bridge between its two installations on opposite sides of a river yet charge a zero accounting price for its use by the various decentralized manufacturing and administrative divisions. (Zero would certainly be the right price if a positive accounting price discouraged the use of the bridge while extra use involved no extra cost.) The bridge considered as a separate

Nor, by the way, is monopoly a satisfactory way out. It is true that in many cases where competition is unworkable—where one or a few firms are bound by reason of scale efficiency to saturate the market—monopolists or a few large oligopolists, so-called, could all make a profit. It may well be, for instance, that there is a positive price at which the operation of our bridge would be profitable, i.e., would more than cover cost. It may even be that such private monopolistic operation is the best of the administratively and politically feasible organizational devices for getting the bridge built and operated. But the fact remains that any such noncompetitive rationing of crossings by a price calculated to maximize net revenue results in less-than-efficient allocation. Bridge crossings would be restricted below the number which would just equate the cost of the last crossing to offer-price. In our example, where marginal cost is zero, some socially *costless* crossings would be discouraged. The output of crossings could be increased without decreasing the output of anything else.[14]

Monopoly, moreover, may not even be a second-best answer, not even with appropriate "discipline" imposed by public agencies staffed by administrators straight out of Plato. It is entirely possible wherever economies of scale are substantial that there is no price which would cover the cost of a facility which nevertheless is required for efficient allocation. It is an old but still intriguing proposition of economics that an activity may be necessary for efficiency though even monopoly operation would fail to cover its cost. The only true test is provided by a perfectly "discriminating" monopolist, so called, who manages for every single crossing to squeeze out of every single customer the maximum toll that the individual is prepared to pay to be permitted that one crossing. The resources that go into a bridge can be shown to be misallocated only if such a perfectly discriminating monopolist, who confronts every user at every crossing with a lump-sum, take-it-or-leave-it offer which reflects a perfect assessment of the customer's desire for that crossing, should fail to cover the cost of the bridge.[15]

The moral of all this is plain. As regards activities characterized

activity would make accounting losses, yet total company profits would be increased.

14. Note that the effect on allocation is quite distinct from what usually worries people about monopoly—its effect on income distribution.

15. Put differently, there exist many situations where no single "admission" price would raise sufficient revenue to cover the cost of an establishment,

by economies of large-scale production (at levels of output which are relevant in terms of the volume of demand), a price-market system, while it may still serve to raise revenue to cover cost, will no longer be simultaneously efficient in rationing output. Alternatively, the price which will efficiently ration output will fail to raise sufficient revenue to avoid loss. Monopolistic operation (at price greater than marginal cost) may or may not succeed in covering cost; where so, however, there will be inefficient curtailment of output. And where not, subsidy may be unavoidable if there is to be any output whatever.

This is the sum and substance of the *qualitative* case, in terms of efficiency, against exclusive reliance on the test of profit as concerns such things as railroads, airlines, roads, public parks, public libraries, river-valley development, and perhaps even the postal services. All these activities are characterized by decreasing unit cost at the relevant levels of output. Competition, in the economist's sense, is not feasible. In some cases monopolistic operation may yield a "full-cost" price, but, since by the very nature of the situation a price which covers unit cost will exceed marginal cost, the result is misallocation. In other cases, there exists no full-cost price, i.e., no price which will yield enough revenue to cover cost, and it is impossible to get any output without subsidy (barring, perhaps, only a very sophisticated structure of differential prices). If we take seriously the case for efficiently catering to consumers' preferences, unadulterated markets will not do.[16]

Where the "Invisible Hand" Fails (2) · Where marginal cost is positive but less than unit cost, efficient allocation (in an ideal world) requires that output be rationed by a price equal to

---

e.g., of a repertory theater company where, however, lump-sum contributions based on an "all plays free or no theater" choice, would, if only people could be made honestly to own up to their preferences, amply cover cost. (The qualification about "owning up" has to do with the problem of "publicness" discussed in the next section.)

16. It does not follow, of course, that we should give up on market mediation in *all* or even most sectors of the economy where decreasing-cost activities predominate. Inefficient markets may often do much better than any feasible alternative mode of organization. (To cite only one reason, subsidies require taxes, which in turn give rise to inefficiency.) The point is only that we cannot count on market decisions to lead to even approximately efficient allocation when it comes to strongly decreasing-cost activities; that to allocate resources to such activities according to their commercial profitability may be exceedingly costly.

marginal cost and that the resulting losses be subsidized. This is typically the situation in so-called public utilities. Additional use entails some additional cost, but the initial fixed cost of the facility, whether it be a port, a dam, a thermal station, or a railroad line, is so high relative to costs which vary with the rate at which the facility is used that unit cost declines with output, and equality of price and marginal cost implies operating in the red.

There are activities, however, where the additional cost of extra use is literally zero. The economist labels the output of such activities "public." A good or service is defined as public if X's consumption of it leads to no subtraction from what is left over for consumption by Y and Z. Radio programs, the services rendered by the beacon atop the Statue of Liberty, the protection provided by the Strategic Air Command are some examples. The additional resource costs of an extra TV viewer, of an extra listener at an uncrowded open air concert, of an additional child watching a fireworks display, of a newly naturalized citizen benefiting from the deterrent-potential of the "Nautilus," of the "Queen Mary" as well as the "Liberté" taking directional guidance from a lighthouse beacon—all are zero. Hence, for efficient allocation, price too must be zero. Pay television may be judged preferable to having to listen to toothpaste advertisements every fifteen minutes, but if it involves charging anyone a positive price for doing something that does not cost anyone else a penny, i.e., for tuning-in, it leads to inefficient allocation (though perhaps less so than does the advertising).[17]

Examples of *pure* public goods are few. Most things, even battleships and certainly open-air concerts and schools (though *not* knowledge), have an "if-more-for-you-then-less-for-me" quality. But this is of little comfort. If a commodity or a service has even a trace of "publicness," be it only in the form of by-product effects

17. Again, the proposition that price must be zero is not a dictum based on intuition but a theorem subject to formal proof. And again, it is subject to the qualification that it *may* in some instances be less inefficient to use the price system to raise the revenue required to cover the cost of a facility than to use taxes (even though this implies charging a positive price that will cause misallocation). But commercial profitability is a very poor indicator of whether a facility whose services are "public" in the technical sense is worth having to start off with. (If the assertion that the theorem about zero price is subject to proof seems puzzling, recall that allocation was defined as efficient if the configuration of inputs, outputs, and distribution corresponds exactly to the solution of a mathematical maximum problem with given constraints.)

which impinge inseparably on many people, then profit- and preference-seeking market calculation will not efficiently mediate its production and distribution. Hence the obvious fact that such things as urban renewal, hospital facilities, education, research, street lighting, vaccination programs, parks, police protection, and the like yield benefits of a "more-for-you-means-no-less-for-me" sort guarantees that market decisions with regard to these activities will fail to do justice to consumers' tastes.

It is sometimes alleged, mistakenly, that the nub of the difficulty lies in the "inability" of a producer of a public good physically to exclude users or to control the rationing of his produce among them, i.e., with "divorce of scarcity from effective ownership." The implication is that if only it weren't impossible, clumsy, costly, or illegal to "keep book" on who produces and who gets what and to enforce payment, all would be well. It is evident that for pure public goods this is not so. It is entirely *feasible* to "own" a bridge, and perhaps profitably to ration crossings; indeed, a private owner would do so. But, as was emphasized above, such profitable rationing, such "compensation" for services rendered, would inefficiently misallocate the output of bridge crossings. If in terms of alternative opportunities the extra cost of an additional crossing is zero, the only price consistent with efficiency is, once again, zero. Ditto for, say, TV programs or that most valuable of assets, new knowledge.[18]

In a sense, as use of the bridge as an example has already implied, a "public good" situation is simply a polar instance of decreasing costs. Yet it leads more directly to the core of the case

18. It would not be impossible, after all, by strengthening patent and copyright protection, to increase substantially the power of the originator to appropriate, i.e., to cash in on, the benefits of a valuable idea. (TV shows, in turn, and also radar-equipped lighthouses, could be protected from free-riders by means of electronic "scramblers.") But it is the essence of public goods that reward by ration price would be inefficient. To be efficient in rationing scarcities the price system must fail in its rewards; and if it is used to reward, it will reward the wrong things.

There are, of course, situations where exclusion is *the* binding consideration, where certain "goods" or "bads" with determinate and "profitable" efficiency prices are not (easily) appropriated. The cost to a producer of training a laborer is a case in point. The social benefit accrues over the working lifetime of the trainee; the private benefit to the producer accrues until the man quits to go to work for a competitor. The "fault" lies in the Emancipation Proclamation and in such imperfections of the capital market as make it difficult for the trainee to borrow in order to invest in himself at rates appropriate to a reasonable estimate of risk and expected return.

for tax-financed government spending than does the ordinary decreasing-cost model. The latter tends to draw one's attention to the problem of motivating producers to produce something the ration price of which, to be efficient, must be less than unit cost. This certainly requires subsidies, but why coercive, mandatory taxation? Why cannot everybody be counted on to contribute according to his anticipation of subjective, own-taste-determined benefit? Moreover, would not the sum raised by such voluntary contributions accurately reflect people's tastes for, say, a mosquito-control program, and hence provide us with just the measure of consumer benefit we need to match against the cost?

Unfortunately, the very condition which gives rise to the need for a subsidy will cause a system of voluntary contributions to misrepresent people's tastes for public goods. Sharing of *private* goods in proportion to voluntary "contributions"—which is precisely what happens where goods are rationed by price in competitive markets—is efficient because a "sensible" economic man's "contributions," his dollar purchases, accurately reflect his preference ordering. He contributes to the financing of apple production, that is, he buys apples, until the last nickel spent on apples yields just enough apples to compensate him for forgoing five cents' worth of nuts and pipe cleaners. He so "reveals" his tastes, however, only because to get apples he must pay for them, because apples will be available to him for consumption in proportion to what he spends. If apples were like firework displays, or mosquito-control programs, or open-air concerts on the neighbor's lawn, in other words, if his consumption of apples were a function not of how many he paid for but of their *total* supply, then his dollar contribution or purchase would hardly reflect his true tastes. Especially if he is one of many, he would be tempted to "understate" his desire for such "apples," i.e., for public goods, in the hope that other people would shoulder a higher share of the cost without his forgoing any of the benefit. Or conceivably, if he is one of a few and if the total cost of the facility relative to his pocketbook is small, he might underestimate others' eagerness and "overpay," ending up, and unnecessarily so, with more of public and less of private goods than he would like. But whether he underpays or overpays—and as regards costly activities (e.g., national defense) the latter is unlikely—the poker-like bluffing and dissimulation intrinsic to the problem of sharing the cost of public goods will cause not only simple allocation by price but also more elaborate systems of financing by voluntary contribution to be grossly unreliable in fixing the balance between public and private goods. It would always be possible, by changing the balance, to do what would never be feasible in a frictionless free-market world of pure private goods—make everyone better off.

We need not pursue the fine detail.[19] The point is clear enough —public good and decreasing cost phenomena cause private market decisions to go wrong. Market prices will fail to approximate true scarcity values in terms of wants; they will be loaded with misinformation, and producers' profit calculations will leave out of account much of the private benefit associated with public goods. The "invisible hand" will fumble: people's decentralized market choices will not efficiently cater to their tastes. If tastes matter, the community must take communal responsibility for the balance between private and public goods. The proposition that government has a significant allocating function turns out to be a corollary of the doctrine of consumer sovereignty.[20]

HOW PUBLIC MONEY IS SPENT

Much of the above would be beside the point if publicly financed activities did not exhibit a strong public quality. It happens, however, that fact and reason suggest otherwise—that the bulk of federal as well as state and local purchases in 1957, for instance, were for services with a strong decreasing-cost public-good quality. *Without implying anything whatever about the detailed project complexion of the various major programs, or*

19. Anyone interested should consult Paul Samuelson's originating development of the theory of public goods in the *Review of Economics and Statistics* (November 1954, 1955, and 1958).

20. The fact that people's market choices do badly by their *own* tastes is a paradox only in a trivial sense. If one adopts the useful fiction of "rationality"—as I have done throughout—a man will by definition so choose as to do the best by his own tastes, *given the environment* (i.e., prices). But he will do so whether the ratio of the price of Cadillacs to the price of lollypops is thirty thousand to one or one to thirty thousand. If the latter price ratio prevailed he would still do the best he could, but since the real opportunity cost of Cadillacs is in fact much greater than that of lollypops, market choices would hardly do well by tastes. If it is the right to choose that matters, any set of prices invented by an O.P.A. man gone berserk would do as well as any other.

For a technical discussion of the various modes and causes of market failure, see my "The Anatomy of Market Failure," *Quarterly Journal of Economics*, August 1958, pp. 351–379.

about the merits of the organizational devices being used, or, most emphatically, about the appropriate quantitative scale of such programs, it is evident that it cannot simply be assumed that market mediation would have done better by people's wants than did public allocation as regards national defense; general government; international affairs and finance; public health and sanitation; education; police, fire-protection, and prisons; regulation of commerce and finance; highway, water, and air transportation; transit, electricity, water, gas, and postal services; and conservation, development, and recreational use of natural resources. In 1957 these categories accounted for 96.8 per cent of public purchases of goods and services [hereafter denoted "G"].

About the other 3.2 per cent ($2.81 billion) of G, horseback judgment is more difficult even in gross qualitative terms, especially since most of the money was used to support programs the primary purpose of which is to provide income compensation to particular groups of people (i.e., to redistribute income). Expenditure on veterans' hospitals and medical care ($813 million, all federal) and on veterans' education and training ($9 million) is clearly of this sort, yet it can perhaps be defended in terms of the public quality of the services rendered. Equivalent cash disbursements to veterans would not have resulted in equivalent allocations to hospital facilities even if veterans' own preferences had called for such allocations. The same is true of the $185 million (all but $9 million of it state-local) that was spent on housing and community redevelopment.[21] On the other hand, the $895 million of G-type expenditure on public assistance and relief and on old-age retirement benefits, etc. (most of it federal-financed state-local spending) is best defended—if it is to be defended—on grounds of income distribution. Preference for services in kind over outright cash grants cannot easily be justified except in paternalistic terms.[22]

21. Housing expenditure yields output that is partially public because people care about the physical character of the neighborhood they and their children's schoolmates live in, and hence at least some of the benefit accrues inseparably to many people.

Some of the $299 million spent on "labor and manpower" (mostly federal-grant-financed state-local G) is also of this sort. It is used in part to cover the cost of administering unemployment compensation and employment service activities, to finance the Bureau of Apprenticeship and Training, etc.

22. It does not follow, however, that it cannot be justified. Few people seriously believe that the world would be a better place if literally *all*

This leaves unaccounted-for $261 million of (net) purchases of goods and services under the "agriculture" rubric and $3.14 billion of federal spending which the Commerce Department labels "subsidies less current surplus of government enterprises." [23] Of this last, $176 million went for highways and water- and air-transport, $9 million for housing and community redevelopment, and $545 million for the postal services—all activities which would fare badly if left to markets. The bulk of the money, however—$2.73 billion of subsidies and the $261 million of G—was accounted for by agriculture, with $2.48 billion going to stabilize farm prices and income.[24] For this, of all major programs, the public-good argument contains no defense. Income maintenance is the prime consideration, and it is a sad commentary on our politics that we have been unable to agree on a less devious and less wasteful means to achieve the desired end.[25]

Agriculture aside, then, free markets would not do well by most of the major functions now served by government. The rule that allocation by markets cannot be improved upon, that shifting of resources from government to private use will necessarily improve allocation, is—or ought to be—dead.

---

paternalistic measures designed to protect people against themselves were scrapped.

23. Plus some $352 million of miscellaneous administrative expenditure labeled as "other," most of it in two categories: veterans' services, and commerce and housing. Incidentally, the percentages are relative to G gross of the $422 million of government sales.

24. Total subsidies exceeded $3.14 billion by the amount of profits earned by federal enterprises.

25. Whether or not the end is justified is a matter of distributional ethics and not economic efficiency. (Ends and means do, of course, interact. The principal reason why we have not been able to work out a less wasteful stabilization program is that people disagree over the proper objectives of such a program. In particular, the major beneficiaries of the present program are quite aware that they cannot possibly gain political acceptance for an equally lucrative but more efficient arrangement such as would identify income redistribution from taxpayers in general to particular people who are now farmers as the objective of the program. And so far, the farm bloc has had enough political power to veto any change that would really hurt.)

Gross G for agriculture was $805 million. Some of this, however, was probably for more or less public activities, e.g., for research, genuine conservation, electrification, etc.

Prices *vs.* Taxes: A Classification of U.S. Public Expenditures

O. H. BROWNLEE

O. H. Brownlee is Professor of Economics at the University of Minnesota. His contribution to a conference of the National Bureau of Economic Research on public finance addresses the question of the extent to which government services can be sold rather than financed by taxes.

ALTHOUGH I favor using price as a rationing device wherever a reasonable opportunity exists, I believe that the appropriate area for application of market pricing to the determination of how much of various goods and services government should produce is a relatively small one. Opportunities undoubtedly exist for financing such items as fire and police protection partially on the basis of service actually rendered. Nevertheless, such cases would be relatively insignificant in terms of the over-all pattern of public expenditure. I see few *major* services that ought to be financed exclusively from sales revenue that are not already being financed in this way. However, charges at less than cost might well be established for some services that are now provided free.

My criteria for evaluating whether a service is being rationed appropriately and whether the amount produced is optimal do not include the effects upon the distribution of income. If agreement could be reached with respect to how various income distributions should be ordered, the best one could be achieved independently of the production pattern of government services.

A virtue of rationing services by the price mechanism is that such a procedure permits obtaining information regarding how users value these services relative to other things that they might obtain. Together with appropriate cost information, such demand data would permit one to determine whether too little or too much of a service was being produced. For services which have no external economies or diseconomies in consumption or production, i.e., the consumption level of one person does not enter directly as a variable in the utility functions of other persons and the production level does not affect the physical productivities of resources in other uses, setting the price equal to marginal production cost and noting whether there is excess demand or excess supply can, under certain conditions, tell one whether too little or too much is being produced—provided, of course, that the optimal level of output is not zero. If there are external economies or diseconomies in production or consumption, services still might be allocated by the price mechanism, but the optimal amount to produce would not be that at which price is equal to marginal cost.

The validity of these assertions and the conditions which must prevail in order for them to be used as the basis for good rules to guide resource allocation are well known. I will not reproduce the "proofs" here. Instead let me try to indicate their applicability to determining which services should be "priced" and how the resulting pattern might compare with the existing one.

CLASSIFYING PUBLIC EXPENDITURES

Among the goods and services that should not be priced are those currently labeled by economists as "public" or "community" goods, i.e., those which can be consumed by one person without a reduction in the quantities available to others.[1] "Voluntary" contributions for the support of such activities will not necessarily be sufficient to obtain the best amounts of them, since there seems to be no reasonable way of inducing persons to reveal their true preferences for such goods relative to others. Although there is no unanimity with respect to which services fall in this class, expenditures for defense and associated activities fit this classification and bulk large in the over-all expenditure pattern.

At the other pole is the class of services produced under conditions of constant or increasing marginal production cost and of a character such that there are neither external economies

1. Paul A. Samuelson, "The Pure Theory of Public Expenditures," *The Review of Economics and Statistics*, November 1954, pp. 387–9; Stephen Enke, "More on the Misuse of Mathematics in Economics: Rejoinder," *ibid.*, May 1955, pp. 131–3; Julius Margolis, "A Comment on the Pure Theory of Public Expenditure," *ibid.*, November 1955, pp. 347–9; Samuelson, "Diagramatic Exposition of a Theory of Public Expenditure," *ibid.*, November 1955, pp. 350–6; Samuelson, "Aspects of Public Expenditure Theories," *ibid.*, November 1958, pp. 332–8.

nor diseconomies of production or consumption associated with them. These should be rationed by price (or a mechanism comparable to the price mechanism), and the output at which the market clears when price is equal to marginal cost is the appropriate one to produce. For the most part, such services are not produced by government except in cases where the cost of collecting from users in accordance with quantities used is high relative to production costs. However, there is no inherent reason why government should not produce such goods providing that it attaches appropriate values to the resources that are used in production, allows for the restrictions that it imposes upon private producers in determining costs *and* does not cover losses from general tax revenues. That one or more of these conditions would be violated is not unlikely.

In between these two extremes are those services which have external economies in consumption and/or decreasing marginal production costs leading inherently to monopoly. Those with pronounced external economies in consumption generally have been produced by government; those with obvious increasing returns generally have been subject to regulation.

A detailed description of governmental services which can be classified accurately according to the three categories suggested— "public goods," services with pronounced external economies in consumption and/or production, and services which should be priced at marginal cost—is not readily available. However, a cursory examination of aggregate data suggests the following somewhat crude allocation of some of the major service categories [in the accompanying table].

The above classification is somewhat arbitrary and does not reveal the things that are of interest in determining whether services are being produced in appropriate quantities. Although it is a picture for only one short period of time, this picture is not an atypical one. Of particular interest is that (1) there are no "sales receipts" from services that benefit both the users and other parties (i.e., have pronounced external economies in consumption)—although some such receipts probably should be attributed to sanitation—and (2) there is a substantial amount of support from general tax funds for a service that I have classified as one that should be sold at marginal cost—higher education. Included in the expenditures for this service are those for research, so that all of the difference between expenditures and receipts should not

Categories of Government Service [a]

	Expenditure (billions of dollars)	"Sales Receipts" (billions of dollars)
A. "Public goods"		
1. Federal government		
a. General government	1.7	
b. National defense, including atomic energy, USIS, mutual security, State Department, and research and development	48.6	
c. Health, hospitals and medical (largely veterans)	2.4	
2. State and local governments		
a. General control	1.7	
b. Public safety [b]		
(I) Police	1.5	
(II) Fire	0.8	
c. Health, hospitals and welfare		
(I) Welfare	3.4	
(II) Hospitals [b]	3.2	
B. Services with pronounced external economies		
1. State and local governments		
a. Elementary and secondary education	11.9	
b. Sanitation		
(I) Sewage	0.9	
(II) Other sanitation	0.5	
C. Saleable services		
1. Federal government		
a. Postal service	4.1	4.0
b. General aids to business	0.2	
c. Higher education	0.45 [c]	
d. Highways		1.0
2. State and local governments		
a. Higher education	1.5	0.4
b. Highways	7.8 [d]	4.0 [e]
c. Public utilities	3.5	2.9
d. Liquor stores	0.9	1.1

[a] Data for the federal government are for 1960, and are from Executive Office of the President, *The Federal Budget in Brief,* Fiscal Year 1960. Those for state and local governments are for 1957 and are from *State and Local Government Finances in 1957,* Bureau of the Census, February, 1957.

[b] Police and fire protection as well as hospitals contain a component that is clearly not in the category of "public goods." However, I prefer to err on the side of making the category of saleable goods too small rather than too large.

[c] Included in state and local expenditure and should not be counted separately.

[d] Includes some capital expenditures that should not be charged exclusively to current services.

[e] Estimated. 1955 fuels taxes and auto, truck, and bus registration fees were $3.65 billion.

be attributed to higher education. Nevertheless, I believe that nearly everyone agrees that tuition receipts at publicly supported institutions of higher education are less than the costs that reasonably could be allocated to the teaching function.

EDUCATION

As I asserted earlier, the fact that a service has external economies associated with its consumption does not imply that it should not be priced. Consider some of the implications of pricing the services of elementary and secondary schools.

Elementary education is a commodity that is believed to have such important effects upon persons other than those who obtain it that it has been made not only free but compulsory. To make persons pay for something which they may not wish to consume generally would not be considered desirable. However, there may be decided advantages to widening the choice of what might be consumed; and there are potential gains from inducing suppliers to minimize the cost of producing whatever they produce. Combining payments to persons conditional upon these payments being spent upon elementary education with institutional arrangements whereby any entrepreneur who meets certain minimum production requirements is qualified as a seller could further both of these objectives.[2] Adoption of such a proposal would not answer the question, "Are we spending the correct amount upon education?" but it would provide a more satisfactory answer to the question of whether that which was being made available was being provided at minimum cost.

Services that benefit persons other than the immediate users could be offered to users at a price below marginal cost or a subsidy could be provided to users, as was suggested above in the case of elementary education. The latter procedure appears to me to be preferred in that it permits a greater element of competition among suppliers. Thus rather than directly providing innoculations, medical examinations, etc., the government might give each person a minimum grant conditional upon its being used for such purposes and let the person select his own supplier.

Let me now turn to the potentialities of the pricing mechanism

2. See Milton Friedman, "The Role of Government in Education," included in Robert A. Solo, ed., Economics and the Public Interest, Rutgers University Press, 1956.

for determining the appropriate production levels for higher education.

The service, higher education, is obtained by consumers because of its impact upon earnings—in which case it can be treated as an investment good—or because the knowledge is desired for its own sake—in which event it can be treated as a consumption good. In either event, I believe that investing in such education is like investing in any other capital asset and that the consumption of higher education by one person does not enter other persons' utility functions.

The statement that one person's consumption of higher education does not enter the utility functions of other persons is an assertion without either adequate proof or disproof.

If my belief is correct, state colleges and universities should receive support from general tax sources only for research; tuition should be raised to cover instruction costs, and the terms under which people can borrow to invest in education should be the same as those under which they can borrow to make other kinds of investments. I am not the sole protagonist of this general proposal and it has by now been widely enough voiced so that I need not develop it further.[3]

We have little information about the demand of educational services so that I can not make a good guess about what the pattern would be if such a proposal were put into effect. However, one would expect the distribution of education to be altered somewhat. Persons now attending college but not willing to pay the full costs would not attend; and persons willing to pay the costs but not now able to obtain funds would attend college. Also one would expect the costs of providing a given level of service to be reduced. Most important of all, the question of whether we need more facilities for higher education could be answered more satisfactorily than it can be at the present time.

Allocating government services by pricing them has limited applicability. To me, an appeal of the price mechanism is that it provides information that would permit us to settle some debates about whether an expenditure is too large or too small. The use of prices in guiding how to produce a given level of service is an area that has not been discussed here. It also offers possibilities for improving resource allocation.

3. See Milton Friedman, *op. cit.*, for example.

Economic Problems in Urban Renewal

OTTO A. DAVIS AND ANDREW B. WHINSTON

This paper is a revised version of a contribution to an interdisciplinary symposium on urban renewal published in Law and Contemporary Problems. *Otto A. Davis is Assistant Professor in the Graduate School of Industrial Administration of the Carnegie Institute of Technology. Andrew B. Whinston is Associate Professor of Economics at the University of Virginia.*

URBAN RENEWAL in this country is predicated upon the notions that the market mechanism has not functioned "properly" in urban property and that governmental action can "improve" the situation. Since welfare economics provides tools for judging market performance and public policy measures, it would not be surprising to find that welfare economics can illuminate the subject of urban renewal.

THE MARKET MECHANISM AND URBAN BLIGHT

Why do individuals fail to keep their properties in "acceptable" states of repair? Several arguments may be advanced to answer this question. For example, it has been asserted that property owners have exaggerated notions of the extent and timing of municipal expansion. Hence they may neglect possible improvements of existing structures in anticipation of the arrival of more intensive uses which bring capital gains. Note that even if this argument is accepted as plausible—and the reason why property owners might have exaggerated notions about municipal expansion is by no means evident—it does not constitute an argument for urban renewal. Instead, one might infer that, given sufficient time, a transition to intensive and profitable uses would take place. Then too, it can be argued that there is no reason to expect governmental authorities to have better judgment than individual entrepreneurs.

Aside from the "mistaken-judgments" argument, it might seem plausible at first glance to believe on the basis of price theory and the profit maximization assumption that urban blight could not occur. After all, would not profit-maximizing individuals find it to their advantage to keep their property in a state of repair? Certainly it seems reasonable to suppose that if individual benefits from repair or redevelopment exceed individual costs, then individual action could be expected and no social action would be necessary. We shall now attempt to demonstrate why rational individual action might allow property to deteriorate and blight to occur.

First of all, the fact that the value of any one property depends in part upon the neighborhood in which it is located seems so obvious as hardly to merit discussion. Yet, since this simple fact is the villain of the piece, further elaboration is warranted. Introspection seems sufficient to indicate that persons consider the neighborhood when deciding to buy or rent some piece of urban property. If this is the case then externalities are present in utility functions; that is to say, the subjective utility or enjoyment derived from a property depends not only upon the design, state of repairs, and so on of that property, but also upon the characteristics of nearby properties. This fact will, of course, be reflected in both capital and rental values. This is the same as saying that it is also reflected in the return on investment.

In order to explain how interdependence can cause urban blight, we introduce a simple example from the theory of games. This example, which has been developed in an entirely different context and is commonly known as "the Prisoner's Dilemma," appears to contain the important points at issue here.[1] For the sake of simplicity, let us consider only two adjacent properties. More general situations do not alter the result but do complicate

1. For an explanation of the "game theoretic" points of interest in the Prisoner's-Dilemma example, see R. Duncan Luce and Howard Raiffa, *Games and Decisions* (New York: John Wiley, 1957). The reason for the intriguing title of this type of game-theory analysis is interesting in itself. The name is derived from a popular interpretation. The district attorney takes two suspects into custody and keeps them separated. He is sure that they are guilty of a specific crime but he does not have adequate evidence for a conviction. He talks to each separately and tells them that they can confess or not confess. If neither confesses, then he will book them on some minor charge and both will receive minor punishment. If both confess, then they will be prosecuted but he will recommend less than the most severe sentence. If either one confesses and the other does not, then the confessor will receive lenient treatment for turning state's evidence, whereas the latter will get "the book" slapped at him. The Prisoner's Dilemma is that, without collusion between them, the rational action for each individual is to confess.

the reasoning. Let us use the labels Owner I and Owner II. Suppose that each owner has made an initial investment in his property from which he is reaping a return, and is now trying to determine whether to make the additional investment for redevelopment. The additional investment will, of course, alter the return which he receives, and so will the decision of the other owner.

The situation which they might face can be summarized in the following game matrix:

Owner II

		Invest	Not invest
Owner I	Invest	.07 .07	.03 .10
	Not invest	.10 .03	.04 .04

The matrix game is given the following interpretation: Each property owner has made an initial investment and has an additional sum which is invested in, say, corporate bonds. At present, the average return on both these investments, the property and the corporate bonds considered together, is 4 per cent. Thus if neither owner makes the decision to sell his corporate bonds and make a new investment in the redevelopment of his property, each will continue to get the 4-per cent average return. This situation is represented by the entries within brackets in the lower right of the matrix where each individual has made the decision "Not invest." The left-hand figure in the brackets always refers to the average return which Owner I receives, and the right-hand figure reflects the return of Owner II. Thus for the "Not invest–Not invest" decision, the matrix entry reflects the fact that both owners continue to get a 4-per cent return.

On the other hand, if both individuals make the decision to sell their bonds and invest the proceeds in redevelopment of their property, it is assumed that each will obtain an average return of 7 per cent on his total investment. Therefore, the entry in the upper left of the matrix, the entry for the "Invest–Invest" decisions, has a 7-per cent return for each owner.

The other two entries in the matrix, which represent the situation when one owner invests and the other does not, are a little more complicated. We assumed, as was mentioned earlier, that externalities, both external economies and diseconomies, are present. These interdependencies are reflected in the returns from investment. For example, consider the entries in the brackets in the lower left corner of the matrix. In this situation, Owner I has decided to "Not invest" and Owner II has decided to "Invest."

Owner I is assumed to obtain some of the benefits from Owner II's investment, the redevelopment contributing something to a "better neighborhood." For example, if the two properties under consideration happened to be apartment buildings, the decision of Owner II to invest might mean that he will demolish his "out-dated" apartment building and construct a new one complete with off-street parking and other amenities. But this means that the tenants of Owner I will now have an easier time finding parking spaces on the streets, their children may have the opportunity of associating with the children of the "higher-class" people who may be attracted to the modern apartment building, and so forth. All this means that (as soon as leases allow) Owner I can edge up his rents. Thus his return is increased without having to make an additional investment. We assume that his return becomes 10 per cent in this case, and this figure is appropriately entered in the matrix. Owner II, on the other hand, will find that, since his renters also consider the "neighborhood" (which includes the ill effects of Owner I's "out-dated" structure), his level of rents will have to be less than would be the case if his apartment building were in an alternative location. Thus we assume that the return on his total investment (the investment in the now-demolished structure plus the investment in the new structure) falls to 3 per cent. This figure is also appropriately entered in the matrix. For simplicity, the reverse situation, where Owner I decides to invest and Owner II decides not to invest, is taken to be similar. Thus the reverse entries are made in the upper right corner of the matrix.

Having described the possible situations which the two owners face, consider now the decision-making process. Both owners are assumed to be aware of the returns which are available to themselves in the hypothesized situations. Owner I will be considered first. Owner I must decide whether to invest or not invest. Remember that the left-hand entries in the brackets represent the possible returns for Owner I. Two possible actions of Owner

II are relevant for Owner I in his effort to make his own decision. Therefore, Owner I might use the following decision process: Assume, first, that Owner II decides to invest. Then what decision will be the most advantageous? A decision to invest means only a 7-per cent return on Owner I's capital, whereas the decision not to invest will yield an average return of 10 per cent of the total relevant amount of capital. Therefore, if Owner II decides to invest, it certainly is individually advantageous to Owner I not to invest. But suppose that Owner II decides not to invest. Then what will be the most advantageous decision for Owner I? Once again the results can be seen from the matrix. For Owner I the decision to invest now means that he will receive only a 3-per cent return on his capital, whereas the decision not to invest means that he can continue to receive the 4-per cent average return. Therefore, if Owner II decides not to invest, it still is individually advantageous to Owner I not invest.

The situation for Owner II is similar. If Owner I is assumed to invest, then Owner II can gain a 10-per cent return on his capital by not investing and only a 7-per cent return by investing. If Owner I is assumed not to invest, then Owner II can gain only a 3-per cent return by investing, but a 4-per cent average return by not investing. Therefore, the individually rational action for Owner II also is not to invest.

The situation described above means, of course, that neither Owner I nor Owner II will decide to invest in redevelopment. Therefore, we might conclude that the interdependencies summarized in the Prisoner's Dilemma example can explain why blighted areas can develop [2] and persist. Before concluding the analysis, however, we might try to answer some questions which may at this point be forthcoming.

THE DESIRABILITY OF COORDINATION OR SINGLE OWNERSHIP

First of all, it might be suggested that we have imposed an unrealistic condition by not allowing the two owners to coordi-

2. It is to be emphasized that these results depend upon the interdependencies or neighborhood effects being "sufficiently strong" to get a combination of returns similar to those which we used in the example. It is unlikely that this condition would be satisfied for all urban property. Our point is that similar combinations seem possible, and if they do occur, then they can explain one peculiar phenomenon of urban property. The explanation is presented later in the paper.

nate their decisions. After all, does it not seem likely that the two owners would get together and mutually agree to invest in the redevelopment of their properties? Not only would such action be socially desirable, but it would seem to be individually advantageous. Note that while it might be easy for the two property owners in our simple example to communicate and coordinate their decisions,[3] this would not appear to be the case as the number of individuals increased. If any single owner were to decide not to invest while all other owners decided to redevelop, then the former would stand to gain by such action. The mere presence of many owners would seem to make coordination more difficult and thus make our assumption more realistic. Yet, this is precisely the point; it is the objective of social policy to encourage individuals in such situations to coordinate their decisions so that interdependencies will not prevent the achievement of a Pareto welfare point. In this regard, it is worthwhile to note that, if coordination and redevelopment do take place voluntarily, then no problem exists, and urban renewal is not needed.

Second, it might be observed that, if coordinated action does not take place, incentive exists for either Owner I, Owner II, or some third party to purchase the properties and develop both of them in order that 7-per cent return can be obtained. And certainly it cannot be denied that this often occurs in reality. However, it is necessary to point out here that, because of the institutional peculiarities of urban property, there is no assurance that such a result will always take place. Consider, for example, an area composed of many holdings. Suppose that renewal or redevelopment would be feasible if coordination could be achieved, but that individual action alone will not result in such investment due to the interdependencies. In other words, the situation is assumed to be similar to the previous example except that many owners are present. Incentive exists for some entrepreneur to attempt to purchase the entire area and invest in redevelopment or renewal.

Now suppose that one or more of the owners of the small plots in the area became aware of the entrepreneur's intentions. If the small plots were so located as to be important for a successful

3. It will be recalled that we made the example overly simple only for the purpose of exposition. While the consideration of many individuals would make the example more realistic, it would only make the game theory more complicated and not alter the result as far as this case is concerned.

project, then the small holders might realize that it would be possible to gain by either (1) using their position to expropriate part of the entrepreneur's expected profits by demanding a very high price for their properties or (2) refusing to sell in order to enjoy the external economies generated by the redevelopment. If several of the small holders become aware of the entrepreneur's intentions, then it is entirely possible, with no communication or collusion between these small holders, for a situation to result where each tries to expropriate as much of the entrepreneur's profit as possible by either of the above methods. This competition can result in a Prisoner's Dilemma for the small holders. Individually rational action on their part may result in the cancellation of the project by the entrepreneur. Indeed, anyone familiar with the functioning of the urban property market must be aware of such difficulties and of the care that must be taken to prevent price gouging when an effort is made to assemble some tract of land.[4]

URBAN "BLIGHT" DEFINED

If the above analysis is correct, then it is clear that situations may exist where individually rational action may not allow for socially desirable investment in the redevelopment of urban properties. Now such situations need not—indeed, in general will not—exist in all urban properties. The results of the analysis not only required special assumptions about the nature of investment returns caused by interdependencies, but it was also shown that, due to the special institutional character of tract assembly, the presence of numerous small holdings can block entrepreneurial action for redevelopment. These two conditions may or may not be filled for any given tract of land. However, we now may use the above results to *define* urban blight.[5] Blight is said to exist whenever (1) strictly individual action does not result

4. For example, Raymond Vernon states, "As the city developed, most of its land was cut up in small parcels and covered with durable structures of one kind or another. The problem of assembling these sites, in the absence of some type of condemnation power, required a planning horizon of many years and a willingness to risk the possibility of price gouging by the last holdout." Raymond Vernon, *The Changing Economic Function of the Central City* (New York: The Committee for Economic Development, 1959).

5. It is to be pointed out and emphasized that our definition of the term "blight" does not seem to be what is meant by the term in common usage where it has a connotation of absolute obsolescence. Our definition refers to

in redevelopment, (2) the coordination of decision-making via some means would result in redevelopment, and (3) the sum of benefits from renewal could exceed the sum of costs. These conditions must be filled. We shall devote a major portion of the latter part of the article to making this definition operational; but, for the moment, let it suffice for us to point out two factors. First, it is a problem of social policy to develop methods whereby blighted areas can be recognized and positive action can be taken to facilitate either redevelopment or renewal. Second, and this point may be controversial, blight is not necessarily associated with the outward appearance of properties in any area.

This second point may be contrary to intuitive ideas about blight. We have defined blight strictly in relation to the allocation of resources. The fact that the properties in an area have a "poor" appearance may or may not be an indication of blight and the misallocation of resources. Several factors, aside from tastes, help to determine the appearance of properties. The situation which we have described, where individually rational action may lead to no investment and deterioration, is only one type of case. Another may be based on the distribution of incomes. The poor can hardly be expected to afford the spacious and comfortable quarters of the well-to-do. Indeed, given the existence of low-income households, a slum area *may* represent an efficient use of resources. If the existence of slums *per se* violates one's ethical standards, then, as economists, we can only point out that for elimination of slums the main economic concern must be with the distribution of income, and urban renewal is not sufficient to solve that problem. Indeed, unless some action is taken to alter the distribution of income, the renewal of slum areas is likely to lead to the creation of slum areas elsewhere.[6] It is to be emphasized that slums may or may

the misuse of land in general and carries no such connotation. The difference in meanings is unfortunate, but we could not find a more appropriate term.

6. It is a curious fact that renewal seems to be regarded as a "cure" for slum areas. For, granted the distribution of income and the fact that the poor simply cannot afford to pay high enough rents to warrant the more spacious and comfortable quarters, the renewal of all slum areas, unless accompanied by an income-subsidy program, would only be self-defeating and lead to social waste. Renewal of all slum areas could cause rents for the "nicer" quarters to fall temporarily within the possible range of the poor, but the rents would not be sufficiently high to warrant expenditures by the landlord to maintain the structure. New slums would appear, calling for

not satisfy the definition of a blighted area. On the other hand, the mere fact that the properties in some given area appear "nice" to the eye is not sufficient evidence to indicate that blight (by our definition) is absent.

PUBLIC POLICY AND URBAN "BLIGHT"

Having seen that, due to externalities or interdependencies and the difficulty of tract assembly, individually rational action may allow blight to develop, we now turn our attention to questions of public policy. It bears repeating that wherever our definition of blight is satisfied, then resources are misallocated in the sense that some institutional arrangement—some means—exists under which redevelopment or renewal could profitably be carried out. The problem is to discover that institutional arrangement. We begin our search by examining briefly the relevant aspects of the present practices.

Title I of the Housing Act of 1949 [7] seems to have set the general pattern for urban renewal practices. While the act of 1954 [8] broadened the concept, the general formula for urban redevelopment remains essentially unchanged. Both federal loans and capital grants are provided for the projects. Loans are generally for the purpose of providing working capital. The capital grants may cover up to two-thirds of the net cost of the project, with the remainder of the funds being provided by either state or local sources.[9]

The striking fact about the present program, and also about many of the proposals for extending that program, is the utter lack of a relevant criterion for expenditures. How much should be invested in urban renewal? How does one determine whether projects are really worthwhile? It is widely admitted that there is a lack of adequate criteria even to determine what projects should be undertaken.

---

more renewal activity. This process would simply continue. On the other hand, efficient slum-removal programs are possible via renewal if care is taken to subsidize the rents of all low-income families.

7. 63 Stat. 413, 42 U.S.C. paragraphs 1441–60 (1958).

8. 68 Stat. 622, as amended, 42 U.S.C. paragraphs 1450–62 (1958); 68 Stat. 596, as amended, 12 U.S.C. paragraphs 1715k, 1715l (1958).

9. There are, of course, conditions which must be satisfied before a community can be eligible for federal funds. See *e.g.*, Commission on Intergovernmental Relations, *Twenty-five Federal Grant-in-aid Programs* (1955).

Having pointed out that existing policies contain no explicit criteria for determining either the amount of public money to invest in urban renewal or when a project is desirable, we now propose two kinds of actions: preventive and reconstructive.

Preventive Action · As was pointed out earlier, the problem in preventing the development of blight consists essentially in finding methods of coordinating the decisions about investment in repair and upkeep so that the socially and individually desirable choices are equated. One step in this direction can be made through the development and use of a special type of building code which bears a superficial resemblance to municipal zoning.[10] It can be seen from the Prisoner's Dilemma analogy discussed earlier that it is desirable for an individual owner to invest *if there is assurance that all individuals will be constrained to make a similar decision.* The special building code specifying minimum levels of repair and upkeep can provide a rough approximation toward optimal levels of coordination.

A brief outline of the scheme follows. Since it is intuitively obvious that different types of property require different kinds of repair and types of upkeep, it would seem desirable that these building codes differ according to the type of property under consideration. The role of the planner would be to try to determine the proper restrictions for each type of property. He could try to gather information on interaction effects through the use of statistical sampling techniques and questionnaires. He then could draw up districts and try to estimate the proper level of the building code for each district. A crude approximation to the benefit-cost criterion is easily supplied. It is advantageous to property owners mutually to constrain themselves to make "appropriate" repair expenditures, for this coordinates decisions. Therefore, the planner can simply submit the proposed code for each district to the property owners of that district; if the planner has proposed an appropriate code, then mutual consent should be forthcoming. If mutual consent is not obtained, then it would seem suitable to assume that the proper code for the

10. It is to be emphasized that the building code envisioned here bears only a superficial resemblance to zoning. The two tools are aimed at different problems. Municipal zoning tries to prevent the establishment of "undesirable" properties in specified neighborhoods. These special building codes would be aimed at the elimination of interdependencies affecting repairs and upkeep decisions.

district has not been proposed and that a new proposal would be necessary.[11]

While codes adopted via the above scheme should be helpful in preventing blight, it must be noted that implementation of this plan would require the selection of an appropriate institutional and legal framework. As economists, we do not pretend to know the legal difficulties that might be involved; but a joint effort by the two professions to set up the framework for such a scheme seems to us to be desirable.

Reconstructive Action · Let us now turn our attention to the policy problem when blight is already in existence. Present practices provide something of a framework here; what is missing is a relevant criterion. Of course, it should be noted that it is sometimes possible to obtain redevelopment through individual effort via the previously stated special-building-code method. In other instances, optimal property uses may have changed from what they formerly were. The area may be composed of lots too small to obtain an orderly transition of property uses by means of the building code. It may be desirable to replan streets, or other reasons may be advanced for the usual type of urban renewal effort. Therefore, let us try to determine the appropriate comparison of costs and benefits when the usual type of renewal activity takes place.

We proceed by imagining a renewal project. Assume that the city government or its renewal authority has marked some blighted area for redevelopment. Taking the property tax rate as given, suppose that the city raises funds for the project by selling bonds. With the money thus raised, the city purchases the blighted area (using the right of eminent domain wherever needed), the outdated structures are demolished, and adequate provision is made for public services. Then, having finished its part of the operation, the city sells lots to entrepreneurs who have agreed in advance to build, say, modern apartment complexes.

11. Our use of the term "mutual consent" may represent something of a subterfuge. In actual practice, it may not be desirable to insist on unanimity nor may a simple majority be enough. Something on the order of 80 to 90 per cent may be reasonable. For a discussion of the problems involved in voting and the difficulties involved in selecting political-decision rules, see James M. Buchanan and Gordon Tullock, *The Calculus of Consent* (Ann Arbor: University of Michigan Press, 1961).

Note what the city's action accomplishes. It removes the obstacles to private renewal. The right of eminent domain removes the possibility of price gouging and stubborn property owners acting so as to prevent the assembly of a large enough tract. Furthermore, each entrepreneur who buys lots from the city is assured that the adjoining lots in the renewal area will also be suitably developed. Recall that in the Prisoner's Dilemma illustration it was the interaction effects which caused the "Not invest–Not invest" decisions to be dominant. Here each entrepreneur is of necessity going to invest according to the plan so that interaction difficulties are eliminated.

One fact needs great emphasis here. *The elimination of externalities or interaction effects causes social and private products to be equated.* Thus this action, which eliminates the obstacles which prevented purely private redevelopment, makes possible the development of a criterion to determine whether the entire renewal project is justified from the point of view of an efficient allocation of resources. We know that it is necessary for social benefit to be greater than social cost for any project to be socially justified. But whereas social benefits and costs generally are difficult if not impossible to measure, the elimination of interaction effects makes it possible for us to use revenues and expenditures as approximate measures. It follows, then, that renewal projects are justified if, and only if, revenues exceed expenditures. This is not to say that it is easy to determine the appropriate revenues and expenditures associated with a renewal project, but it is to say that the better we determine them, the closer will our approximate measures come to social benefits and costs.

What are the appropriate revenues and expenditures? The expenditures of the local governmental authority include the acquisition of land, demolition and improvements, aiding in the relocation of displaced tenants,[12] and the present value of interest payments. Of these items, the expenditure associated with the acquisition of land is the more troublesome because public bodies are likely to own some parcels in any renewal area. For some of these parcels—*e.g.*, lots with out-dated structures such as old public office buildings—values can be estimated by com-

12. Peculiarly enough, the present-day requirement that individuals be paid for their property and the administrative rule of aiding individuals who are dislocated to find new quarters affords a method of approximate compensation so that the Pareto criterion can be applied.

paring them with private lots and structures in the area. For other types of public properties—e.g., streets and playgrounds—estimates of the social values are much more difficult and arbitrary. However, it is important that prices be assigned to all parcels in the renewal area, regardless of whether or not the city's redevelopment authority actually has to purchase these parcels, and that all "accounting transfers" between governmental agencies in addition to actual expenditures be included in the figure for the total cost of the project. Only if expenditures are estimated in this manner will they approximate the social costs of the project.

In regard to revenues, the primary item is receipts from the sale of lots. But here the situation is complicated by two factors. Not only must estimates be made of the social worth of public projects such as parks, playgrounds, public buildings, streets, and so forth, and the values of these counted as receipts from the project; but since property taxes almost always are utilized by local governments and since the discounted value of the tax is likely to be shifted onto the immobile resource—land—it is necessary to take this factor into account. If the project is successful, the new structures should have a higher value than the old ones; so there should be a net addition to tax revenues. This net addition should be discounted to a present value and counted as a receipt from the project in order to prevent revenues from understating the social worth of the redevelopment.[13]

If the above procedures are followed, the revenues-expenditures criterion should closely approximate the benefits-costs criterion, depending especially, of course, upon how well the social benefits derived from special public projects are estimated. But even with the difficult estimation problems, which are not unique to urban renewal but are involved in all publicly provided goods and services, the criterion of approving renewal projects if, and only if, revenues exceed expenditures should result in an approximately efficient utilization of urban land.

Several corollaries to the revenues-expenditures criterion

13. Of course, care must be taken when the total acreage of publicly owned property in the renewal area changes because of the project. Publicly owned land and structures are not subject to the property tax, and this factor must be taken into account when the tax-exempt acreage changes. The important point is that property taxes cause prices to understate the social value of the properties so that when a change in tax status is granted, the figure for the net change in tax revenues has to be adjusted accordingly.

should be pointed out. From the point of view of an efficient utilization of land resources, no federal or state subsidies are needed for urban renewal purposes *per se*, although governmental support of public projects and services associated with urban renewal is required, just as this support is needed when these are not associated with renewal. But on the basis of the outlined methods of estimating revenues and expenditures, urban renewal projects should not lose money. Indeed, they should result in a profit. On the other hand, constitutional and/or statutory debt limits which are often imposed upon local governments should be waived for borrowing for urban renewal purposes. Finally, local governments should be granted the right to use the power of eminent domain for the purpose of urban renewal.

Summary and Concluding Comments · This essay has examined certain aspects of the market in urban property in an effort to determine why blight can develop and persist. We have seen that strong interdependence effects can explain both the appearance and continued existence of this phenomenon. Yet, the fact that sufficient interdependence may cause individual and market allocations to be something less than optimal for certain parts of urban areas does not mean that present-day renewal practices are the best possible. Indeed, the present-day practices are aimed at only one aspect of the problem. In our examination of this issue we have proposed a program designed to prevent the occurrence of urban blight so that the need for renewal programs will be lessened. Furthermore, for those areas where blight does exist and the preventive program is not practical, it is possible to state a criterion for investment in urban renewal. This criterion—that investment should take place if and only if (appropriately measured) revenues exceed expenditures—is an approximation to a social benefits-costs criterion. It is admitted that our present institutions may not make it easy to carry out these two schemes, but, granted the increasing importance of this problem, an effort toward its solution seems to be more and more urgent.

Reflections on Public Expenditure Theory

WALTER W. HELLER

Walter W. Heller, Professor of Economics at the University of Minnesota, submitted this essay to the Joint Economic Committee hearings on public expenditures. From 1961–1964, he was chairman of the President's Council of Economic Advisers.

WHAT DOES the economist have to offer a perplexed public and its policymaking representatives on the theory of Government functions as they affect the budget? The cynic's offhand answer, "not much," may be close to the mark if one demands definitive rules of thumb for determining the precise scope of Government functions and level of Government expenditures. But if, instead, the demand is for economic guidelines to aid the budgetary decisionmaker (1) in blending rationally the service, stabilization, and income-transfer functions of Government, (2) in identifying those deficiencies in the private-market mechanism which call for Government budgetary action or, more broadly, those activities where Government use or control of resources promises greater returns than private use or control, and (3) in selecting the most efficient means of carrying out Government functions and activities (whether by Government production, contracts with private producers, transfer payments, loans, guaranties, tax concessions, and so forth)—if this is the nature of the demands on him, the economist is prepared to make a modest offering now and to work along lines that promise a greater contribution in the future.

In a sense, this paper is a progress report designed to show where the economist can already offer some useful counsel, to indicate some of the lines along which promising work is being done, and to suggest certain limitations or constraints within which the economic criteria for dividing resources between public and private use must be applied.

A BASIC FRAMEWORK

As a first step in the search for economic guideposts, we need to disentangle, classify, and define the basic objectives and functions of Government that shape its budgetary decisions. Fortunately, Prof. Richard A. Musgrave has developed a conceptual framework for this task in his "multiple theory of budget determination." [1]

The component functions of the budget as he brings them into focus are: (1) The service, or want-satisfying, function: to provide for the satisfaction of those individual wants which the market mechanism cannot satisfy effectively (e. g., education and conservation) or is incapable of satisfying (e. g., defense and justice); (2) the income-transfer or distributional function: to make those corrections in the existing income distribution (by size, by occupational groups, by geographical area, etc.) which society desires; and (3) the stabilization function: to join with monetary policy and other measures to raise or lower the level of aggregate demand so as to maintain full employment and avoid inflation. The first function is of dominant interest [here] and the succeeding sections of the paper return to it. But several general implications of the Musgrave system as a whole deserve attention before turning to specifics.

Musgrave's formulation helps unclutter our thinking on the component parts of the budget decision. It drives home the significant point that our decisions on how much and what kind of want-satisfying services to provide by Government budgets need not be tied to our demands on the budget for correction of either the existing patterns of income distribution or the level of aggregate demand. If we prefer, we can have a small budget for services (financed by taxes levied on the benefit principle) combined with a big budget for redistributive transfers of income (financed by taxes levied on the ability principle), or vice versa; and either combination can be coupled with either a deficit to stimulate demand and employment or a surplus to reduce demand

1. See, for example, "A Multiple Theory of Budget Determination" *Finanzarchiv* 1957, vol. 13, No. 3, pp. 333–343, and the relevant chapters of his treatise, *The Theory of Public Finance* (New York: McGraw-Hill, 1959).

and check inflation. In this respect, it is reminiscent of Samuelson's "daring doctrine" that by appropriate fiscal-monetary policy "a community can have full employment, can at the same time have the rate of capital formation it wants, and can accomplish all this compatibly with the degree of income-redistributing taxation it ethically desires.[2] Musgrave, in turn, points the way to achieving any combination of Government services, income redistribution, and economic redistribution, and economic stability we set our sights on.

So far, so good. The waters, though deep, are clear and relatively still. They get somewhat muddied and troubled when we move from the clear-cut want-satisfying programs (subject to the benefit principle) and clear-cut distributive programs (subject to the ability principle) into dual-purpose programs, transfers-in-kind in the form of subsidized housing, medical care, vocational education, and so forth. For here we are no longer furnishing services that the majority has voted to meet its own needs (including both selfishly motivated needs like defense and police protection and socially motivated needs like foreign aid) via Government, but are in effect requiring the minority to accept services which they might or might not have bought had they been handed an equivalent amount of cash. Perhaps they would have preferred to spend it on wine, women, and song, but the majority is apparently saying, "No, we know what's best for you." Can this be justified?

It may be digressing to do so, but let us consider for a moment the provision of free vocational education as a case in point. It might be argued that vocational training results in a direct increase in earning power of the trainee (since employers will be willing to pay him higher wages) and that it should therefore be left in private hands or, if furnished publicly, should be financed under the market principle (by direct charges to the recipient of the service) rather than the budget principle (provided free of charge and financed by general taxation).[3] In terms of the service budget alone, the foregoing conclusion is probably

2. Paul A. Samuelson, "The New Look in Tax and Fiscal Policy," in *Federal Tax Policy for Economic Growth and Stability,* Joint Committee on the Economic Report, Washington, November 9, 1955, p. 234.

3. For a discussion of these principles see Gerhard Colm, *Essays in Public Finance and Fiscal Policy,* New York, 1955, pp. 8–11.

right. But bringing in the redistributive motive puts subsidized vocational training in a different light. The voting majority may feel that income transferred in this form constitutes a more efficient and desirable form of transfer than a direct cash transfer. It insures that the transferred economic power won't be squandered in foolish and dissolute ways. It approaches reduction of economic inequality through greater equality of opportunity. In the process, it strengthens the economy's productive capacity.

The new welfare economics may protest that this is a form of tyranny of the majority of the voters over the minority, that each individual is his own best judge of his welfare. Since the equivalent cash payment would have been spent differently, it is said to be a violation of consumer sovereignty. But it is also quite possible that the recipient of the transfer in kind will vote with the majority to have this kind of program rather than a direct cash payment. The individual may accept and welcome the discipline in such an arrangement which overcomes his own self-deplored lack of willpower (a lack which is not restricted to children, aged persons, and imbeciles). How many of us would "prefer" to spend our time quite differently than we do if left to our own devices, yet are willing to accept, or even welcome, the tyranny of a deadline as a condition of participating in a desirable project? Seen in this light, the transfer in kind may interfere more with license than with freedom of consumer choice. I do not mean to dismiss the "tyranny" argument, but its force is certainly softened by the kind of consideration just examined. It may be further softened if we accept the proposition that the responsibility of the voters' representatives goes beyond a mere recording of individual preferences to leadership and education designed to redirect individual preferences along lines which a social consensus deems more constructive.

Even beyond this, the transfer in kind may actually have a large service component, i.e., secondary benefits which accrue to others than the direct recipient of the service.[4] For example,

4. To the extent that the income transfer motive is the sole or dominant motive for keeping certain services on the public budget (or at least causing us to supply them on the budget principle rather than the market principle), a rise in average family income and a decline in inequality will eventually bring us to a point where programs such as vocational education and low-cost housing should be moved off of the Government budget and

low-income housing may confer indirect benefits on high-income people in surrounding areas for which they are willing to pay a considerable price. Subsidized housing projects may replace unsightly slums, arrest urban blight which threatens to encroach on better neighborhoods, and reduce fire and police protection costs. To this extent, taxes on high-income people to subsidize low-cost housing may in large part be a payment for the indirect benefits they receive rather than a transfer payment. Clearly identifying and separating the service elements from the redistributive element in this manner suggests that the wants of third-party beneficiaries are being satisfied by using the direct recipient of subsidized housing, medical care, education and the like as the instrument, willing or unwilling, for this purpose.

This formulation may also shed new light on the theory of progressive taxation. Musgrave suggests that high-income people may be willing to pay proportionately more for a given government service than low-income people (i.e., the income elasticity of demand for the service is greater than unity), even in the case of government services like defense and justice which by their nature must be consumed in equal amounts by all persons. Add to this consideration the important indirect stake which the upper income groups have in subsidized programs for the lower income groups (i.e., programs not equally consumed by all). The direct beneficiary may put a low value on the service and a high value on money, while the indirect beneficiary (who gets secondary benefits in protection from epidemics, in arresting of urban blight, in a more stable body politic and labor force, and so forth) may put a relatively high value on the service and a low value on money. The tax policy result: progressive taxation on the benefit principle.

---

into the market economy. This point is undoubtedly much more distant for some programs than others. Also, I do not mean to suggest that the main impact of economic growth and prosperity is to reduce Government expenditures. Both in the case of intermediate public goods (such as roads), the demand for which typically moves in accord with private goods, and in the case of "end item" services (such as better education and recreation), the demand for which increases with higher standards of living, economic growth and prosperity mean higher rather than lower demands for Government services. (See Gerhard Colm, "Comments on Samuelson's Theory of Public Finance," *The Review of Economics and Statistics*, November 1956, vol. 38, p. 410.)

ECONOMIC DETERMINANTS OF THE PROPER SPHERE OF GOVERNMENT ACTIVITY

Given a framework for straight thinking about budget functions, the economist is brought face to face with two questions that come closer to the central problem of the proper sphere of Government activity. First, where competitive bidding via the pricing mechanism is inapplicable, how are the preferences of voters for governmental services to be revealed, measured, and appropriately financed? Second, waiving the question of measurement of preferences, where would the line between public and private control over resources be drawn if economic efficiency were the only criterion to be implied?

On the first question, insofar as it relates to individual preferences for public goods, economists have agreed on the nature and difficulty of the problem, have made some intriguing suggestions as to its solution, and have concluded that it is next to insoluble. The key difficulty is that the voting process, unlike the pricing process, does not force the consumer of public goods to show his hand. The essence of preference measurement is the showing of how much of one good or service the consumer is willing to forgo as the price of acquiring another. But the amount of a public good or service (say, of defense, police protection, or schooling) available to the voter is independent of the amount he pays in taxes or the intensity of his demand for it.[5] Unless and until we devise a reliable and reasonably accurate method of detecting specific voter preferences in some detail, our definition of the proper sphere of government activity will have to rely chiefly on the informed judgment and perception of those whom we vote into legislative and executive office.[6]

5. For an illuminating exploration of ways and means to get at a more valid and clear-cut expression of voter preferences for government services, see the pioneering work by Howard R. Bowen, *Toward Social Economy*, New York, 1948, especially ch. 18, "Collective Choice." In this chapter Bowen explores both voting and polling techniques for ascertaining those individual tastes and preferences which cannot find expression in, or be measured by, the market mechanism.

6. Insofar as voter wants in the public sphere go beyond individualistic preferences to general welfare choices (as Colm, in his article commenting on Samuelson's theory, argues that they not only do, but should), the

This being the case, the economist's task is to contribute what he can to this informed judgment and perception. In effect, the economist's job becomes one of telling the voters and their representatives what their preferences as to governmental activities would be if they were guided by the principle of economic efficiency. In doing so, the economist is not proposing that decisions as to what kinds of activities should be assigned to government—what wants should be satisfied and resources should be redirected through government action—should be made on economic grounds alone. He is fully aware that values such as those of political and economic freedom play a vital role in these decisions. But he can perform the valuable service of identifying those deficiencies in the market mechanism and those inherent economic characteristics of government which make it economically advantageous to have certain services provided by government rather than by private initiative. In other words he can show where government intervention in resource allocation and use promises a greater return per unit of input than untrammeled private use.

The economist recognizes, of course, that there are areas in which he is necessarily mute, or at least should not speak unless spoken to. These are the areas of pure public goods, whose benefits are clearly indivisible and nonmarketable, and no amount of economic wisdom can determine the appropriate levels of output and expenditure.[7] In the realm of defense, for example, one successful Russian earth satellite or intercontinental ballistics missile will (and should), outweigh 10,000 economists in determining the appropriate level of expenditures. At most, the

---

problem changes form, but the desirability of sharper definition of voter preferences remains undiminished.

7. No attempt is made here to define a public good. Samuelson (in "The Pure Theory of Public Expenditures," *The Review of Economics and Statistics*, November 1954, vol. 36, p. 387) has defined "collective consumption goods" as those in which one individual's consumption of the good leads to no diminution of any other individual's consumption of that good. McKenna [in an unpublished paper.—*Editor*] would broaden the definition to include as public goods all those that provide "benefit simultaneously and automatically to more than one member of society." It would seem that while the former definition leaves out many goods provided under the budget principle, McKenna's embraces quite a number provided under the market principle. [For a discussion of public goods see the essay by Bator in this volume. *Editor*.]

economist stands ready to offer analysis and judgments as to the critical levels of defense expenditures beyond which they threaten serious inflation in the absence of drastic tax action or curtailment of civilian programs, or, given that action, threaten impairment of producer incentives and essential civilian programs.

A much more fruitful activity for the economist is to demonstrate the economic advantage offered by government intervention, budgetary and otherwise, in those intermediate service areas where benefits are at least partially divisible and marketable. A number of economists have made useful contributions on this front.[8] In what situations does economic logic point to government intervention to correct the market mechanism's allocation of resources in the interests of greater efficiency in their use?

1. Where there are important third-party benefits [usually known as neighborhood effects, external effects, or externalities] which accrue to others than the direct beneficiary of the service as in the case of education, disease prevention, police and fire protection, the market price and demand schedules underestimate the marginal and total social benefits provided by the service in question. By and large, the direct beneficiaries are the only ones who enter the private market as buyers, with the result that the services would be undervalued, underpriced, and underproduced unless Government entered the transaction. Government is the instrument for representing the third-party beneficiaries and correcting the deficiency of the market place (though this is not to deny that private religious and philanthropic organizations, for example, also represent third-party beneficiaries and operate on budget rather than market principles).

2. Just as there may be indirect benefits not reflected in market demand, there may be indirect costs inflicted on society which do not enter the private producer's costs and therefore do not influence market supply. Classic examples are the costs of smog,

8. See, for example, O. H. Brownlee and E. D. Allen, *Economics of Public Finance*, second edition, New York, 1954, ch. 10, "The Role of Government Expenditure." See also Max F. Millikan, "Objectives for Economic Policy in a Democracy" (especially pp. 62–68), and Robert Dahl and Charles E. Lindblom, "Variation in Public Expenditure," both in *Income Stabilization for a Developing Democracy*, Max F. Millikan, editor, New Haven, 1953.

water pollution, denuding of forests, and the like. In these areas, private output will exceed the optimum level unless government corrects the situation either by regulation or by a combination of expenditure and charge-backs to the private producers involved.

3. Where a service is best provided, for technical reasons, as a monopoly (e.g., postal service, electricity, railroad transportation), the Government is expected to step in either by regulation or operation to avoid costly duplication and improve the quality of service. Ideally, its function would also be to guide prices toward levels consistent with optimum output. Involved here is the problem of the decreasing cost industry, where efficient plant size is so large relative to total demand that average cost decreases as output increases, and the market solution of the output and price problem will not result in best use of the productive assets. To push production to a point representing an ideal use of resources may require, if not Government operation, a subsidy financed out of tax revenues.

4. Government may enjoy some advantages in production or distribution which make it an inherently more efficient producer of certain services. Here, the classic case is highways, streets, and sidewalks. By providing them free to all comers, Government effects substantial savings in costs of distribution since it does not have to meter the service and charge a price for each specific use. In this category we might also fit projects, such as the initial development of atomic energy, which involve such great risks and huge accumulations of capital that the private market does not have the financial tools to cope with them.

ALTERNATIVE MEANS OF CARRYING OUT GOVERNMENT FUNCTIONS

Given the decisions as to the appropriate sphere of Government activity (on the basis not merely of considerations of greatest economic gain but also of value preferences), there remains the problem of choice among alternative methods to implement these decisions, to achieve given aims and satisfy expressed public wants. This choice will affect the budget in different ways. It may increase expenditures, decrease revenues, establish contingent liabilities, or perhaps have no effect on the budget at all (except for a small amount of administrative expenses involved in the supervisory and regulatory activities). Since the operational question is not merely what functions and activities Government should carry out, but what budgetary principles and expenditure levels these lead to, the problem of implementation must be included in any applied theory of public expenditures.

Here, the economist's role is to determine the most efficient method of providing the service or otherwise influencing resource allocation. He is concerned with minimizing costs, i.e., achieving the stated objective with a minimum expenditure of resources. Needless to say, other considerations will also influence the selection among alternative means, as even a brief consideration of the types of choices involved in the implementation process will make clear.

What are these choices? Take first the case of direct satisfaction of individuals' public wants. Should the Government produce the desired public goods or obtain them from private industry by purchase or contract? To accomplish redistributive ends, should the Government provide transfers in cash or transfers in kind? [9] Should Government rely on public production of educational services, or should it consider private production combined with earmarked transfers of purchasing power to parents? Thus far, the choices all involve direct budgetary expenditures, the level of which differs, at least marginally, depending on the relative efficiency of the method chosen. But in making his choice, the policymaker must consider not merely the direct costs of providing the service but whether one method involves more or less disturbance of private market incentives and patterns of production than another, whether it involves more or less interference with individual freedom (which is largely a function of the extent of Government expenditures and intervention but certainly in part also a function of the form of that intervention), and so on.

Another set of choices may take the item off of the expenditure

9. One involves so-called resource-using (also called factor-purchase or exhaustive) Government expenditures, i.e., payments in exchange for current goods and services rendered, with direct control of resources remaining in public hands. The other involves transfer payments, i.e., payments made without any provision of current goods and services in return, with direct control over resources passing into private hands. [The distinction is discussed in the Introduction to this volume. *Editor.*]

side of the budget entirely, or leave it there only contingently. Should such subsidies as those to promote oil and gas exploration, stimulate foreign investment, expand the merchant marine, promote low-cost housing, and increase the flow of strategic minerals take the form of (1) outright subsidies or above-market-price purchase programs, (2) Government loan programs, (3) Government guaranties, or (4) tax concessions? The choice will clearly involve quite different impacts on Government expenditures.

In many of these cases, the economist can be helpful with his efficiency criterion. But one would be naive to think that efficiency alone dictates the choice. The economist may show that a direct subsidy could stimulate a given amount of private direct investment abroad or a given amount of exploration for oil and gas, with a much smaller cost to the budget than is implicitly required in the tax concession method of achieving the same end. Yet, the costlier tax concession method may be preferred for two simple reasons: (1) it is virtually self-administering, involving no administrative hierarchy to substitute its authority for relatively free private decisions, and (2) it does not involve an increase in the expenditure side of the budget, a fact which has certain attractions to the Executive and Congress.

As yet, no clear boundary lines have been drawn among the various forms of Government intervention to mark off those that properly belong within the scope of public expenditure theory. But this illustrative review of the various choices makes clear that some forms of Government activity which are not reflected in expenditures at all (tax concessions) or only contingently (guaranties) are an integral part of such expenditure theory. In fact, there may be a stronger case for embracing these in expenditure theory than many Government activities which require budgetary outlays but are conducted on the pricing principle, i.e., Government enterprise activities.

Economists are conducting some provocative inquiries into questions of alternative methods of carrying out Government programs in areas where the answers had heretofore been taken for granted. For example, the transfer of schooling to a private production and Government transfer payment basis has been urged by Professor Milton Friedman as a more efficient means of providing the desired service.[10] Professor O. H. Brownlee is currently probing further into this question, as well as the possibilities of transferring other publicly produced services into the sphere of private production.[11] Once fairly conclusive findings are devised as to the methods most likely to minimize costs, there remains the vital task of blending these findings with the nonmonetary values that would be gained or lost in the process of transferring from public to private production.

SOME CONSTRAINTS ON THE APPLICATION OF SPECIFIC ECONOMIC CRITERIA

Repeatedly in this discussion, the note has been sounded that, in determining the level of Government activity, the policymaker cannot live by economics alone. More particularly, we need to guard against setting up our economic guides solely in terms of those considerations which lend themselves to sharp economic analysis and definition. In other words, the role of both economic and noneconomic constraints must be given full weight.

The former include a host of considerations relating particularly to economic motivation in Government versus private undertakings. Government may, for example, have a decided edge in the efficiency of distribution or be able to achieve a better balancing of social costs and social benefits in a variety of fields. Yet, there may be important offsets to these economic advantages in terms of (1) bureaucracy, (2) lack of the profit criterion to gage the results of Government activities, and (3) undesigned or unintended (presumably adverse) economic effects of taxation.[12]

10. See Milton Friedman, "The Role of Government in Education," in *Economics and The Public Interest,* Robert A. Solo, editor, New Brunswick, 1955, pp. 123–144. In his prescription, Friedman would, of course, have Government regulate the private schools to the extent of insuring that they meet certain minimum standards in their programs and facilities.

11. [See the essay by Brownlee included in this volume for his analysis of government roles in education. *Editor.*]

12. These less sharply defined economic effects have to be balanced, of course, against comparable and perhaps offsetting drawbacks in the market mechanism. For an exploration of some of these factors, both in the private and the public sphere, see Robert A. Dahl and Charles E. Lindblom, *Politics, Economics, and Welfare,* New York, 1953, especially pt. V. See also C. Lowell Harriss, "Government Spending: Issues of Theory and Practices," *Public Finance,* vol. 12, 1957, pp. 7–19.

The latter factor, in particular the fact that tax financing of public services involves breaking the link between an individual's cost of a given service and his benefit from it, may involve important offsets to economic advantages otherwise gained by Government expenditure. Thus far, to be sure, no dire consequences of the disincentive effects of taxation have been firmly proved, but changes in the form of private economic activity to minimize taxes are certainly a cost that must be weighed when netting out the balance of economic advantage in Government versus private performance of services.

Beyond the economic factors, one encounters an even more basic and less manageable constraint, namely that of freedom of choice. Thus, it is quite conceivable that following the kinds of economic criteria discussed earlier in the paper would take us considerably farther in the direction of Government spending and control over resource allocation than we would wish to go in terms of possible impairment of economic and political freedom. This consideration enters importantly not merely in decisions as to the proper range of Government activity but also in choosing among alternative methods of providing Government services.

This is not to imply that all value considerations run counter to the expansion of the Government sector of our economy. Such expansion may serve a number of social values, such as greater equality of income and opportunity, a more acceptable social environment, and so on.[13]

To get all of these considerations into the decision-making equation on private versus public provision of a particular service, or on the choice among alternative forms of providing the service, requires a wisdom which goes well beyond the field of economics. Perhaps this explains why so few economists enter politics.

13. This type of consideration is examined in William Vickrey, "An Exchange of Questions Between Economics and Philosophy," in *Goals of Economic Life*, edited by A. Dudley Ward, New York, 1953, pp. 148–177. See also Max F. Millikan, op. cit.

The Tenable Range of Functions of
Local Government

*George J. Stigler is Walgreen Professor of American Institutions
at the University of Chicago. He was one of the panelists appearing before a Congressional subcommittee who contributed papers to the compendium* Federal Expenditures for Growth and
Stability.

The members of the legislative, executive, and judiciary departments
of 13 and more States, the justices of peace, officers of militia, minis-
terial officers of justice, with all the county, corporation, and town
officers, for 3 million and more of people, intermixed, and having particular acquaintance with every class and circle of people, must exceed, beyond all proportion, both in number and influence, those of
every description who will be employed in the administration of the
Federal system (*The Federalist*, No. 45).

THE PRESERVATION of a large role in governmental activity for
local governments is widely accepted as an important social goal.
No one can doubt that the individual citizen gains greatly in
political dignity and wisdom if he can participate in the political
process beyond casting a vote periodically. It is also generally
conceded that a good political system adapts itself to the differing
circumstances and mores of different localities, or, as I would
wish to rephrase it, the system should allow legitimate variations
of types and scales of governmental activity to correspond with
variations in the preferences of different groups of citizens.

Nor will it be denied that this social goal is being increasingly
sacrificed. In 1900, virtually all questions of housing, public
health, crime, and local transportation were dealt with exclusively by State or local governments, and the role of the
Federal Government in education, regulation of business practices, control of natural resources, and redistribution of income

was negligible. Today the Federal Government is very active in each of these areas, and its share of responsibility is gradually increasing.

I propose to examine some of the reasons which are given for the growing centralization of political processes. The proper range of activities of government in general will not be raised. Our question is simply this: If the people in a given community wish to embark on a particular governmental policy, when does the efficient discharge of this policy require that it be imposed by a central authority also upon other communities?

In many minor areas of governmental activity no real questions are raised, as yet, about the feasibility of local sovereignty. If a given community wishes to have superb library facilities, it can build and pay for them; if another community wishes instead a skating rink, it may so choose. If individual citizens in any community disagree strongly with the majority preferences, they may move to a more congenial community. Since governmental functions must often be provided upon a considerable scale to be tolerably efficient in execution, a sufficiently eccentric individual may not be able to find any community with enough like-minded individuals to be able to adopt that series of governmental policies which would exactly suit his taste. For example, he may wish to live in a community with gravel streets and a magnificent observatory, and find no community willing to provide this combination. This sort of limitation is also encountered in consuming the products of private enterprise—I may not find precisely the automobile or typewriter that suits me.

In most areas of governmental activity, however, it is increasingly felt that local governments are inefficient units. When any of three types of governmental activity are sought, it is said that the unit of effective administration must be large in scale—

    1. When the object of a regulatory policy can be nullified by the competition of (including migration to) other local governmental units.

    2. When the source of revenue of the activity can escape financial responsibility by migration to another unit.

    3. When the policy is incapable of efficient performance upon a local scale.

We consider these problems in turn.

THE PROBLEM OF COMPETITION

Suppose that a community wishes to set a high standard of factory safety, and requires the installation of a very expensive safety device. Then the local portion of a much larger industry will be undersold in the common market by factories in other communities, provided they do not also simultaneously set as high standards of safety practices. The local branch of the industry then dies or migrates. These facts can be taken as data for our discussion.

The essence of this argument is that competition, which usually works so well in the area of private enterprise, serves to defeat desirable goals in the area of government. If every governmental unit, save one, were to desire and require elaborate safety devices in the factories of some industry, it is claimed that their desire could be stultified by the presence of the exceptional community which did not have this desire, because the regulated industry would migrate to this community and escape regulation, and the knowledge that it would do so is often enough to prevent the various communities from attempting to regulate it.

It may be remarked that a similar argument is often encountered in the private-enterprise sector. Plants with low wage rates, it is often said, force plants with high wage rates to reduce their wages in order to compete successfully in the common market. In this case the argument is reversible: the plants with high wage rates force plants with low wage rates to raise their wages in order to compete successfully for workers in the common labor market. Both formulations, however, are singularly uninformative, for they do not lead directly to the correct conclusion, which is that the wages of all (similar) workers must approach equality in all plants under competition, and the common wage rate will be governed by the value of the worker's services in those plants which can pay this rate. Can it be that some parallel obscurity attaches to the customary formulation of the unfortunate effect of competition among governments?

The governmental analysis is, in fact, incomplete. Suppose any community set the required level of safety practices as high as it wishes, and then gave a subsidy to each enterprise in the locality equal to the additional cost that these safety devices imposed upon the enterprises. Then there would be no tendency for the local industry to be handicapped in competition with other areas with lower safety standards, and the community would enjoy more worker safety and less of other things than other communities. If 47 percent of the localities or 99 percent of the localities embark upon this policy, then 47 or 99 percent of the factories will have the desired safety practices, and the nonconformist competitors will not have the slightest tendency to injure or attract these safe and expensive factories.

When a community imposes the safety regulations without giving a compensating subsidy, its troubles arise from the fact that it is seeking to push these higher costs off on consumers, and neither local nor distant consumers wish to assume this burden. The problem of competition resolves itself into an unwillingness of the community to bear the costs of its policy when they are posed as an explicit burden.

A similar analysis holds when the community wishes to require of some consumer good that it be of unusually high quality. If it specifies that only goods of this unusual quality be sold in the community, the producers will be quite eager to meet the specifications—at a remunerative price.

Although it involves a digression, it may be profitable to discuss more generally our example of factory safety devices because the discussion will serve to illuminate the workings of competition in general. If workers are faced with the choice of working in one plant, unequipped with safety devices, at an hourly rate of $1.50 but with expected losses from injuries of 5 cents per hour, and in another plant with safety devices they are offered $1.46 with no expected losses from injuries, we should expect them to choose the latter plant. If under these conditions they do not choose the safer plant, the most probable explanation is that they do not correctly appraise the expected losses from injuries and the remedy is to inform them of the consequences of working in factories unequipped with safety devices. In a fully competitive system the entrepreneurs will supply at cost all the safety devices that the workers demand, and all safety devices which return (to the worker, in terms of reduced injuries) as much or more than the cost will be adopted. It may well be that in this situation there will be safety devices which do not pay but which would reduce injuries further, and that the community as a whole sets a higher value on avoidance of these injuries than the workers themselves do. Some moral philosophers might argue that these workers should set a higher value on the avoidance of injuries, but the workers do not, and in a society with free choice of occupation they cannot be made to pay for more safety than they wish. Hence the society must bear the costs of achieving more safety, and the sole question is whether the costs be borne by consumers through compulsory installation of the safety devices and restriction of supply; or by direct grant from public funds.

The competition of other communities as tax collectors is an important form of the alleged difficulty arising out of competition. Suppose community A wishes to have splendid and expensive schools, streets, housing, poor relief, and what not. If it levies sufficient taxes to finance this elaborate program, a large portion of the tax base (industries and well-to-do individuals) will leave the community while simultaneously a large number of beneficiaries of the generous program may immigrate. The tax rates on the narrower tax base will have to be prohibitive (from the viewpoint of the remaining taxpayers) to finance the sumptuous program.

Again we can accept the facts, with one temporary amendment. Let us assume that the same income is received by every family, and no questions of income redistribution are involved. Will the presence of communities with lower tax rates defeat the ambitions of community A? The answer is clearly in the negative. There will be some redistribution of population among communities: those people who prefer cheaper public services and lower tax rates will move elsewhere, and others with opposite taste will move to A. Competition of communities offers not obstacles but opportunities to various communities to choose the types and scales of governmental functions they wish. The proviso that all family incomes are equal has a vast influence on this argument, of course, and we turn now to income redistribution as a goal.

THE DISTRIBUTION OF INCOME

If all families had equal (real) income, would there be any need for local governmental units? Why could not each city be a private corporation, supplying at a price the services its dwellers demanded? With many, many such corporations, competition would prevent monopolistic pricing, and schooling and police and fire protection would be sold at a price including a fair rate of return on investment. This scheme would obviously be inappropriate where the service must be a monopoly (like national defense) and probably also where the community size was so large (due to the economic advantages of size) that the communities were too few to rely upon competition, but let us put these instances aside. We are not seeking to prove that there should be no government, but rather to find the logic of government at the multiunit governmental level.

A basic deficiency in this private-enterprise organization of social life, we would all agree, is that it allows excessive freedom to the individual. It would allow parents to horsewhip children, and it would create communities populated chiefly with drunkards and drug addicts—although thieves would presumably prefer to live among honest men (even with their policemen) than only with other thieves. Public opinion would curb many undesirable personal actions, but the society would wish to compel observance of its basic values. As a result, we must recognize the need for political units large enough so their numbers include enough normal people to insure the imposition of the society's basic moral standards on local communities. Our States —with one or two possible western exceptions—meet this condition of statistical large numbers.

The second basic weakness—some will call it a strength—of the private enterprise organization of local government is that it would not permit price discrimination; it does not have the ability to redistribute income. The purely competitive organization of local services would make it impossible for a local government to obtain money from the rich to pay for the education of the children of the poor, except to the extent that the rich voluntarily assumed this burden.

How can local governments cope with this problem? If 99 communities tax the rich to aid the poor, the rich may congregate in the hundredth community, so this uncooperative community sets the tune. Here competition does not perform with its usual excellence, for competition is the system calculated to organize only voluntary activity.

What is the correct amount of redistribution of income in light of the society's desires? It is more than the unrestricted competition of tax-free colonies of the rich would allow, but less than the most aggressively egalitarian community would desire. The decision must be in some sense a national decision, for the proper amount of redistribution, even if rich and poor were chained to their communities, could not depend upon the accidents of income composition of a particular community. And once this level of redistribution is set, no one community may complain if its rich citizens migrate when it seeks to go above this level of distribution unless the society is prepared to let the most egalitarian community set the scale of income redistribution.

Since redistribution is intrinsically a national policy, it should not be restricted to a community level; a community consisting only of poor people should receive the desired minimum social services. Hence, in pure principle, the Federal Government should collect the progressive levies and redistribute them (in whole or in part) to local units with each unit receiving an amount governed by the number of its poor and the degree of their poverty.

Given this system of tax revenue redistribution, the local governments could still be allowed to perform any function which they were competent to perform efficiently. One community might choose to spend more on schools and less on hospitals than another, but this is surely an area of legitimate freedom; there is no "correct" distribution of expenditures among such functions.

In a society which has no serious program of income redistribution (even as a means to the attainment of minimum goals), local governments would face no basic revenue problems because of competition.[1] It is in keeping with this argument that a century ago almost all functions were local and the problem of competition for the tax base was negligible. With an appropriate fiscal system we could restore these revenue considerations to a position of unimportance even in an era of extensive income redistribution. There still remains the question of whether the local governments could efficiently perform the enlarged range of functions that modern governments have assumed. We turn now to this question.

1. Perhaps a qualification should be entered with respect to the growth of taxable wealth that escapes a general property tax. In England the desire of property owners to ease their tax burdens was a force in the emasculation of local government; see E. Cannan, *The History of Local Rates in England*, second edition, 1912, ch. VI.

THE ECONOMIES OF SCALE

How large must a governmental unit be to perform efficiently the activities which the public wishes governments to perform? This is an area which deserves much more attention than it appears to have received, and the following remarks are highly tentative.

There is a set of functions which are intrinsically national because they are indivisible. The greatest of these is national defense, and it would be ill-served if each State or local unit were to undertake the defense of its own area. One may cite also foreign relations, the national governmental machinery, and the control of relationships among lower governmental levels.

In addition to such traditional functions, one may list certain functions which are or can be performed at a local level but which must be coordinated to achieve efficiency in their design. The transportation systems of localities must take some account also of the needs of long-distance transportation. The radio and television stations of various localities must not jam one another. These are functions which in the economist's language, have large external economies or diseconomies accruing to the areas which do not participate in their execution, so it is essential that they be formulated (although not necessarily administered) on a larger area than the local government.

We should reserve for the Federal Government those functions which are much more efficiently discharged on the largest scale. When local performance involves large duplication, it is inefficient. Thus it seems undesirable to have 48 estimates of wholesale prices since the price movements in most regions will be parallel; on the other hand, the calculation of cost-of-living indexes might suitably be removed from the Bureau of Labor Statistics to the States.

The optimum scale of performance has tacitly become identified with the National, or at least the State, scale almost without examining the nature of the governmental functions under discussion. This seems most surprising to the student of industrial organization; he is accustomed to finding that the activity in an industry with a complex technology is usually efficiently conducted by a firm smaller by almost any measure than the government of a town of 25,000. Is there some special characteristic of governmental functions that makes large units necessary to efficiency?

Only one characteristic seems a possible candidate for this role: the great variety of functions performed by even the small governmental units. The lack of specialization is pronounced even though political scientists complain of a multiplicity of overlapping local units (many of which were established to evade tax or debt limits on local units). Some of these functions can be performed efficiently on a very small scale. Many of the most distinguished private schools and colleges are much smaller than the school system of a town of 5,000 people. Others are more varied. A police department can efficiently control local traffic on a small scale; in one sense it must be worldwide to have an efficient "missing persons" bureau.

But this variety of function is not really unusual. Every enterprise must use goods and services, or produce goods or services, which must be produced or sold on a much wider scale than the enterprise itself can undertake. Even a huge department store is not large enough to make its own delivery trucks, or to print the newspapers in which it advertises. Just as cooperation in these matters is brought about by the price system, so cooperation among governmental units has been developed— and could be carried much further—to avoid the determination and execution of all public functions by that governmental unit which is most efficient in conducting the function with the largest scale of operation.

It happens, as we have already noticed, that one function of paramount importance must be conducted on a very large scale: the collection of revenues designed to redistribute income. Much centralization, in fact probably most centralization, has been a consequence of this situation. A central government is loath to make grants without exercising a degree of control over the local units which disburse the funds. No degree of control less than 100 percent, however, is sufficient to guarantee local performance exactly as the central authorities wish it, and there is no obstacle except tradition to slow down their gradual extension of controls.

The case for imposing controls over the smaller units receiving grants, however, is far from general. The central disbursing authority has no monopoly of wisdom. The State boards of education have imposed a series of certification requirements on local teachers, for example, that have done much to lower the quality of elementary education in the United States. When central governments have superior civil servants, as they often do, the cause lies more often in their control of finance and authority than in the advantages of centralization. It may be true that when most administrative units are small the ablest men cannot conduct affairs on the largest scale, but this seems an odd consideration to give weight in setting the functions of local governments in a democracy. More often the complexity of the tasks at the national level has reached such levels that not the ablest men can control them efficiently.

If grants were given to local governments without supervision, there would be some instances of gross neglect or venality and more variety in the quality of the performance of public functions. We should also expect to find that much of this variety was eminently sensible, and that many types of experimentation would constantly be embarked upon by the more venturesome and the more foolish communities—with large social benefits from both the successes and the failures.

If we give each governmental activity to the smallest governmental unit which can efficiently perform it, there will be a vast resurgence and revitalization of local government in America. A vast reservoir of ability and imagination can be found in the increasing leisure time of the population, and both public functions and private citizens would benefit from the increased participation of citizens in political life. An eminent and powerful structure of local government is a basic ingredient of a society which seeks to give to the individual the fullest possible freedom and responsibility.

Suggested Further Readings

American Assembly, *Atoms for Power* (Prentice-Hall, 1958).

Arrow, Kenneth, J., "Uncertainty and the Economics of Medical Care," *American Economic Review* (December 1963).

Bator, Francis M., *The Question of Government Spending* (Harper, 1960).

Baumol, William J., *Welfare Economics and the Theory of State* (Harvard, 1952).

Black, Duncan, *The Theory of Committees and Elections* (Cambridge, 1958).

Bowen, Howard R., *Toward Social Economy* (Rinehart, 1948).

Break, George F., "Income Tax and Incentives to Work: An Empirical Study," *American Economic Review* (September 1957).

Brownlee, O. H. and W. W. Heller, "Highway Development and Financing," *American Economic Review* (May 1956).

Buchanan, James M., "Politics, Policy and Pigovian Margins," *Economica* (February 1962).

———, and Gordon Tullock, *The Calculus of Consent,* (Michigan, 1961).

Clark, John M., *Alternative to Serfdom* (Knopf, 1948).

Committee for Economic Development, *The Budget and Economic Growth* (1958).

———, *Paying for Better Public Schools* (1958).

———, *Guiding Metropolitan Growth* (1960).

Dahl, Robert A. and Charles E. Lindblom, *Politics, Economics and Welfare* (Harper, 1953).

Downs, Anthony, *An Economic Theory of Democracy* (Harper & Row, 1957).

Fabricant, Solomon, *The Trend of Government Activity in the United States Since 1900* (National Bureau of Economic Research, 1952).

Fellner, William J., "Politics, Economics and Recession," *Yale Review* (1959).

Friedman, Milton, *Capitalism and Freedom,* (Chicago, 1962).

———, "The Role of Government in Education," *Economics and the Public Interest,* ed. by R. Solo (Rutgers, 1955).

Galbraith, J. K., *The Affluent Society* (Houghton Mifflin, 1958).

Gulick, Luther H., *The Metropolitan Problem and American Ideas* (Knopf, 1962).

Hansen, Alvin H., *Economic Issues of the 1960's* (McGraw-Hill, 1961).

Hayek, F., *The Road to Serfdom* (Chicago, 1944).

Hirschleifer, Jack, J. C. DeHaven, J. W. Milliman, *Water Supply: Economics, Technology and Policy* (Chicago, 1960).

Hitch, Charles J. and R. N. McKean, *The Economics of Defense in the Nuclear Age* (Harvard, 1960).

Johnson, Harry G., *Money, Trade and Economic Growth* (Allen and Unwin, 1962).

Keezer, Dexter, ed., *Financing Higher Education, 1960–1970* (McGraw-Hill, 1959).

Krutilla, John V., and Otto Eckstein, *Multiple Purpose River Development* (John Hopkins, 1958).

Lerner, Abba P., *The Economics of Control* (Macmillan, 1944).

Machlup, Fritz, "The Division of Labor Between Government and Private Enterprise," *American Economic Review* (March Supplement, 1943).

McKean, Roland N., *Efficiency in Government through Systems Analysis* (Wiley, 1958).

Musgrave, Richard A., *The Theory of Public Finance* (McGraw-Hill, 1959).

"The Nation and Its Industry in Space," *Fortune* (June 1962), special issue.

Rivlin, Alice M., *The Role of the Federal Government in Financing Higher Education* (Brookings, 1962).

Rothenberg, Jerome, *The Measurement of Social Welfare* (Prentice-Hall, 1961).

Samuelson, Paul A., "Diagrammatic Exposition of a Theory of Public Expenditure," *Review of Economics and Statistics* (November 1955).

Schumpeter, J. A., *Capitalism, Socialism and Democracy*, 3rd ed. (Harper, 1953).

Shenfield, A. A., "The Public Sector versus the Private Sector in Britain," *Modern Age, 6*, No. 1 (Winter 1961–62).

Simon, Herbert A., and Clarence E. Ridley, "The Criterion of Efficiency," *Annals of the American Academy of Political and Social Science* (September 1938).

Somers, Herman M. and Anne R., *Doctors, Patients and Health Insurance* (Brookings, 1961).

Tiebout, Charles M., "A Pure Theory of Local Expenditures," *Journal of Political Economy* (October 1956).

Tullock, Gordon, "Problems of Majority Voting," *Journal of Political Economy* (December 1959).

Turnbull, John G., C. A. Williams, and E. F. Cheit, *Economic and Social Security*, 2nd ed. (Ronald, 1962).

U.S. Congress, Joint Economic Committee, *Federal Expenditure Policy for Growth and Stability* (1957).

Wallich, Henry C., *The Cost of Freedom* (Harper, 1960).

Weisbrod, Burton A., *The Economics of Public Health* (Pennsylvania, 1962).

Williamson, J. G., "Public Expenditure and Revenue: An International Comparison," *Manchester School*, (January 1961).